MONTY PYTHON: COMPLETE AND UTTER THEORY OF THE GROTESQUE

Edited by John O. Thompson

1982
BFI Publishing

British Library Cataloguing in Publication Data

Thompson, John O.
Monty Python: complete and utter theory of the grotesque
1. English wit and humor - History and criticism
I. Title
827'914'09 PR937

ISBN 0 85170 119 1

Published by the British Film Institute
127 Charing Cross Road
London WC2H 0EA

Cover design: Bryan Brown

Typeset by Sprint Productions Ltd,
139 High Street, Beckenham, Kent

Printed in England by Centurion Print of Hertford

CONTENTS

ACKNOWLEDGMENTS

The editor and publisher would like to acknowledge the following for their kind permission to reprint copyright material:

Daily Telegraph (Syndication): for 'Cleese Profile' by William Davis, extract from review of *Time Bandits* by David Castell, 'John Cleese's participation in ITV's *At Last the 1948 Show'* by Philip Purser, and 'The Circus that Flew' by Bevis Hillier. *Financial Times* for review of *Monty Python's Life of Brian* by Nigel Andrews. *TNL Syndication* for reviews by Alan Brien of *Monty Python's Life of Brian* (18 November 1979) and *Jabberwocky* (3 April 1977), Hunter Davies on John Cleese's Childhood (6 March 1977), George Perry on Gilliam and the Middle Ages (27 March 1977), Martin Roth on Python in Japan (3 March 1980), from the *Sunday Times,* and Michael Watts's 'Interview with Terry Gilliam' (16 July 1981), from *The Times,* © Times Newspapers Ltd. The *Observer* for review of *Life of Brian* by Philip French, and article on *Do Not Adjust Your Set* by George Melly. The *Guardian* for 'Monty's Double' by Lee Langley, article on Terry Jones and interview with John Cleese by Alex Hamilton, 'The Python's Tale' by Jonathan Sale, and 'Tinkling Symbols' (unsigned). *Sunday Express Magazine* and the author for 'Not to be Confused with Monty Python' by John Walker. The *Sun* for review of *Monty Python and the Holy Grail* by Romany Bain. The *New Standard* for 'Terry Jones' by Charles Spenser and review of *Time Bandits* by Alexander Walker. The *Daily Mail,* London, for review of *Time Bandits* by Margaret Hinxman, and 'The Secret World of John Cleese' by Chris Greenwood. *Morning Star* for review of *Time Bandits* by Virginia Dignam. *Western Mail* for article referring to *Monty Python's Life of Brian* (21 April 1980).

Variety for 'Lutheran Broadcast Slam at "Life of Brian": crude, rude', by Robert E.A. Lee. *Spectator* for extract from review of *Monty Python's Life of Brian* by Peter Ackroyd. Reviews of *And Now for Something Completely Different* by P.D. Zimmerman and of *Monty Python and the Holy Grail* by Richard Schickel, courtesy of *Time Magazine,* © Time Inc. 1972 and 1975. *The Bookseller* for 'Ten Years of Silly Publishing' by Geoffrey Strachan. *The New Yorker* for 'And We'll Be Back After This Message' and 'Light-years Ahead of the Cuckoo Clock' by Penelope Gilliatt, © 1972 and 1975 The New Yorker Magazine, Inc.

Gay News for interviews with Graham Chapman (1972 and 1980). *Rolling Stone* for 'The Persecution of Monty Python's Life of Brian' by Paul Gambaccini and 'Monty Python's Holiday in the Sun' by Steve Pond, © 1979 and 1980 by Straight Arrow Publishers, Inc. *Esquire* for review of *And Now for Something Completely Different* by Thomas Berger. *Film Comment* for 'Bandit: Terry Gilliam interviewed' by Anne Thompson, © 1981 by Film Society of Lincoln Center. *Wide Angle* and the author for 'Sawing through the Bough: *Tout va bien* as a Brechtian film' by Kristin Thompson. *The Journal of Aesthetics and Art Criticism* for extracts from 'Defining the Grotesque: An Attempt at Synthesis' by Michael Steig.

Associated Book Publishers Ltd. for extracts from Philip Thomson, *The Grotesque.* The Johns Hopkins University Press for extracts from Susan Stewart, *Nonsense: Aspects of Intertextuality in Folklore,* © 1978, 1979. George Weidenfeld and Nicolson Ltd. for extract from Terry Jones, *Chaucer's Knight.* Oxford University Press for extracts from *The Grotesque in English Literature* by Arthur Clayborough, © Oxford University Press 1965. Tavistock Publications, Editions du Seuil and W.W. Norton for extracts from Jacques Lacan, 'Aggressivity in Psychoanalysis' in *Ecrits: A Selection,* tr. Alan Sheridan. The Hogarth Press and Seymour Lawrence, Inc. for extracts from Melanie Klein, 'Some Reflections on *The Oresteia*', in *Our Adult World and Other Essays,* reproduced in *Envy and Gratitude and Other Works.* The MIT Press, Cambridge, Mass, for extracts from Mikhail Bakhtin, *Rabelais and His World,* tr. Helene Iswolsky.

INTRODUCTION

This dossier brings together – perhaps 'jumbles' would be a better word – two sorts of material: interviews with members of the Monty Python team and reviews of their productions on the one hand, and 'theory of the grotesque' extracts on the other.

The element in Python humour which makes the grotesque a useful concept to apply to it was caught by Alexander Walker, reviewing *And Now For Something Completely Different* in the *Evening Standard* (30 September 1971), who noted how well Terry Gilliam's animations survive transplantation from television to the cinema: 'Blown up to billboard dimensions, the marble busts, cardboard dummies and Victorian worthies have a fie-fo-fum menace, more threateningly funny than ever. He's best when he draws blood . . . .' That the threatening can be funny is itself rather strange on the face of it; but the particular form this paradox takes here is very different from, say, Pinteresque 'comedy of menace' effects. Childhood ('fie-fo-fum'), the body ('blood'), and a monstrous juxtaposing or collageing of incompatible elements seem all to be important determinants of the fun, though the relationship among them is far from obvious. This is the realm of the grotesque.

The term 'grotesque' is derived from the Italian for 'caverns' or 'chambers', *grotte*; ultimately its etymology takes us back to the Greek *krypté*, a vault (cf. 'crypt'), *kryptein*, to hide (cf. 'cryptic'). Neil Rhodes (*Elizabethan Grotesque*, London, 1980), writes:

> The word appears in Europe after the discovery in Rome during the early sixteenth century of ancient apartments decorated with bizarre animal and plant formations. As these rooms were, by this time, all underground, they were called caves or 'grottoes' and their decoration, grotesque.

He quotes Vasari (*Lives of the Painters*) on how the style favours

> all kinds of absurd monsters, formed by a freak of nature or by the whims and fancies of the workmen, who in this kind of picture are subject to no rule, but paint a heavy weight attached to the finest thread which could not possibly bear it, a horse with legs of leaves, a man with crane's legs, and any number of bumble-bees and sparrows; so that the one who was able to dream up the strangest things was held to be the most able.

A contemporary Roman description-cum-denunciation of the style is to be found in the treatise *De Architectura*, written by Vitruvius while Augustus was Emperor.

> All those motifs which are based on reality, have now been forsaken for an injudicious fashion. For monstrosities are painted on the walls rather than clear pictures of real things. Instead of columns, fluted stems are painted; instead of gables (*fastigia*), panels with curling leaves and volutes. Candelabra likewise support painted edifices (*aediculae*). On their gables frail flowers, on which random little figures sit, grow in tendrils from their roots. And the slight stems actually bear half-figures, some with human heads, others with the heads of beasts. Such things however, do not exist, never will and never have existed, either. . . . For, in point of fact, how can a stalk support a roof, or a candelabrum bear the ornaments suitable to a gable? How can such a weak and flimsy tendril support a figure sitting on it, and how can flowers and half-figures grow piecemeal out of roots and tendrils?
>
> [Quoted by Clayborough – see section 21 below]

Hostile critics of Monty Python sometimes sound like Vitruvius brought to life again.

Very broadly the case *for* the grotesque can be made on psychoanalytic, sociological or formalist grounds. We shall encounter representatives of each of these positions in what follows. Fortunately, a dossier editor doesn't have to make firm decisions about which position should dominate the discussion; but the reader should be warned that the 'theory' side of the enterprise brings together views that may well be actively incompatible. On the journalism side, the warning is more mundane: press coverage of the Pythons often tells us more about the press than about the Pythons.

I haven't attempted to present materials chronologically, largely because Python history has been very adequately covered in two recent books: Roger Wilmut's *From Fringe to Flying Circus* (London, 1980) and – recounting the tangled tale of the Pythons' various brushes with censorship – Robert Hewison's *Monty Python: The Case Against* (London, 1981), despite its title a fiercely pro-Python document. On the radio comedy background to the Python phenomenon, Barry Took's *Laughter in the Air* (London, 1976; revised edition 1981) is also well worth consulting. All these books are not only lucid but very funny. In keeping with my brief, I have tried to make this dossier not so much funny as grotesque.

JOHN O. THOMPSON

For their help in assembling this dossier, I'd like to thank especially the following: Bill Beard, Jill Cox, Lucy Douch, Gillian Hartnoll, Lynette Hunter, Steve Newman, Geoffrey Nowell-Smith, Richard Paterson (the project's 'onlie begetter'), Steve Pinhay and Ann Thompson, as well as the staff of the BFI's Library Services and the Sydney Jones Library, University of Liverpool.

1 FERRET

The Monty Python team – Graham Chapman, John Cleese, Terry Gilliam, Eric Idle, Terry Jones and Michael Palin – got together in 1969. Cleese and Chapman had worked together before, most recently on ITV's *At Last the 1948 Show* (1967). Philip Purser in the *Sunday Telegraph* remarked on John Cleese's participation in particular; the series ended with 'Cleese as soloist (a rather thin tenor) in the elaborate oratorio "I've Got a Ferret Sticking Up My Nose" '.

He brings to a logical conclusion several trends which have been growing more evident every year – not only that the funny man need no longer *look* funny (Cleese looks like an accountant who in his spare time is a bit fierce on the tennis court) but also that the comic's job is to remain absolutely normal in some bizarre reversal of ordinary circumstances, indeed not even to notice it. The joke about the oratorio on intranasal infestation was that it was every bit as meaningful and profound and mystical to this performer as 'Messiah' is to Sir Malcolm Sargent.

Sunday Telegraph, 26 March 1967.

2 THE VERY IMAGE OF REDEMPTION

Twelve years later, the Python team had, in the eyes of many, brought the Messiah into question much more painfully. In America, the Reverend Patrick J. Sullivan SJ, director of the Catholic Conference's Office for Film and Broadcasting (OFB), issued a measured statement (reported in *Variety*) concerning *Monty Python's Life of Brian*.

He said the OFB is reluctant to use the word 'blasphemy' in describing the film's cardinal sins, terming it 'too restrictive a construct, since I don't know that the Monty Python people went into this with the thought of blaspheming. As we perceive it, the film is blasphemous in its effect, though probably not in intent.'

Even so, Sullivan said, 'it's still very difficult for anyone to explain away the film's final image', in which a string of crucified victims sing a nihilistic ditty suggesting that life is ultimately worthless.

'Having a song explicitly contrary to the Judeo-Christian concept of man's value juxtaposed against the very image of redemption (the cross) becomes something intolerable', he stressed.

. . . He also noted that 'other sensibilities have been bypassed' by the film, 'which does a great deal of ridiculing at the expense of the handicapped.' . . .

Variety, 29 August 1979.

3 ENGLISH AS COLD TOAST OR THE *GUARDIAN*

The sense that there might be something genuinely intolerable about certain Python moments is not universally shared. One of the harshest of *Life of Brian*'s English reviews, by Peter Ackroyd in the *Spectator,* took the opposite tack: the Pythons, television-scale entertainers, aren't up to either blasphemy or the cinema.

Although more rich in intellectual life than *On the Buses,* more playfully oblique than *Up Pompeii,* it suffers from the same delusion: that there is really no distinction between television and the cinema. The camera here lingers on the 'funny walks'; the action is broken down into a number of 'routines', which have all the inner coherence of an obituary column . . . .

There is no doubt about the Englishness of the enterprise; it is as Anglo-Saxon as cold toast. Monty Python humour consists in being naughty without being interestingly offensive; in being knowing rather than clever; in being obvious rather than imaginative. The film does acquire a certain manic energy, but it is of the kind one associates with *Carry On* films. The funniest scene in the entire picture hovers around a Roman character known as 'Biggus Dickus' who has a wife called 'Incontinentia'. At these points, the dialogue sounds as if it has been kidnapped from *Carry On Cleo* and tied down – and so does some of the acting, too.

Spectator, 17 November 1979.

Philip French, in the *Observer,* liked the film, but in its defence suggests something similar.

Few of [the jokes] could be called genuinely blasphemous, for the film lacks the passion of blasphemy. The comedy doesn't have the wry, bruised resignation of Jewish humour. Nor is there any of that Catholic fascination with the liturgical and the sacerdotal one meets in the anti-clerical joking of Continental film-makers like Fellini, Pasolini and Bunuel.

What the Pythons' humour suggests is a class of English public school cynics, C of E to a man, falling about at what they're being asked to take seriously . . . .

Observer, 11 November 1979.

For a more positive view of what the Pythons are if they're not blasphemous, we can turn to Nigel Andrews in the *Financial Times* and Alan Brien in the *Sunday Times.* Andrews usefully points us in a more formalist direction.

You name the lapse of taste, *Monty Python's Life of Brian* perpetrates it. Yet the blasphemy-invoking fuss that surrounded the film in America is for fishers of red herrings only. The Python team have never specialised in made-to-shock 'bad taste', and they do not do so here. That kind of inverted evangelicism – speciality of the world's Lenny Bruces – is way wide of the mark in viewing their any-grist-to-the-mill surreal comedy. What Cleese, Palin, Idle and Co. dispense is the mad concatenation of opposite ideas: their New Testament is a hunting-ground not for caustic iconoclasm but for a helter-skelter flood of anachronisms, non-sequiturs and Pythonesque incongruity.

Financial Times, 9 November 1979.

Brien, evoking some of *Brian*'s funniest moments, brings out the libertarian, *Guardian*-like ethic of the film. (But note how a certain physical disquiet, via the theme of amputation, governs the second paragraph's associative progress from the film's settings to the Ayatollah; and how odd it is to dismiss the faithful's protests as simply the result of their individual 'arbitrary labelling' of 'things' – the crucifixion? – as sacred.)

It manages to be simultaneously a connoisseur's parody of a Hollywood King-of-Kings epic and a sharp dig at splinter-left revolutionaries who ignore the occupying Romans in the rivalry between the People's Front of Judea and the Judean People's Front ('Whatever happened to the Popular Front, Reg?'; 'He's over there.') It includes polemics against racial propaganda from any source ('the Leader who will save Israel by ridding it of the scum of non-Jewish people, making it pure – no foreigners, no gypsies, no riff-raff'); and against capital punishment even endorsed by a criminal hanging upside-down ('If we didn't have crucifixion this country would be in a right bloody mess I can tell you'). It is a full-scale demonstration of the idiocies of conformity ('I say you are the Lord, and I should know, I've followed a few') . . . .

The film usually looks all too real, soaking up some grainy authenticity from the old Zeffirelli sets and settings in Tunisia, a landscape littered with the usual Pythonesque rubbish of severed limbs, squashed animals, unspeakable victuals and grisly instruments. Blasphemous, it probably is to some, since those who arbitrarily label things sacred must expect others to profane them – every cartoonist in Fleet Street would nurse a missing hand under the jurisdiction of Ayatollah Khomeini.

Sunday Times, 18 November 1979.

4 BRAVE SIR ROBIN

In *Monty Python and the Holy Grail* there is an episode in which a knight is 'followed by a small retinue of MUSICIANS in thirteenth-century courtly costume' who sing the following song to keep up his courage:

Bravely good Sir Robin, rode forth from Camelot,
He was not afraid to die, oh brave Sir Robin,
He was not at all afraid to be killed in nasty ways,
Brave brave brave brave Sir Robin.

He was not in the least bit scared to be mashed into a pulp
And have his eyes gouged out and his elbows broken;
To have his kneecaps split and his body burned away
And his limbs all hacked and mangled, brave Sir Robin.

His head smashed in, and his heart gouged out,
And his liver removed, and his bowels unplugged,
And his nostrils raped, and his bottom burnt off,
And his penis split . . . and his . . .

At this point Robin shuts them up: 'Er, that's . . . that's enough music for a while, lads.'

5 DEFINING THE GROTESQUE

Michael Steig's 'Defining the Grotesque: An Attempt at Synthesis' (*The Journal of Aesthetics and Art Criticism* 29, 1970, pp. 253-60) attempts to distinguish psychodynamic processes at work in our enjoyment of the grotesque from those animating neighbouring genres.

Thomas Cramer has enunciated a principle which is crucial to the definition of the grotesque I wish to develop here: 'the grotesque is the feeling of anxiety aroused by means of the comic pushed to an extreme', but conversely, 'the grotesque is the defeat, by means of the comic, of anxiety in the face of the inexplicable'. This formulation of the complementarity of the fearsome and the comic allows us to move beyond the rather mechanical notion of the comic as solely a defensive measure against anxiety: in the grotesque they are more complexly related, in that the extravagant use of the comic can *create* anxiety, as well as relieve it.

Steig continues by likening the grotesque to Freud's notion of the uncanny.

The basic problems . . . seem to be determining the typical sources of the anxiety aroused by the grotesque; analyzing the role of the comic in arousing or allaying anxiety; and deciding how these characteristics distinguish the grotesque from the tale of terror or horror, on the one hand, and from comedy, on the other. Freud provides a possible answer to the first of these questions in his paper, 'The "Uncanny" ' ('*Das "Unheimliche"* '), in which he poses the question of what accounts for the particular effect that leads us in our language to distinguish an area of the uncanny 'within the boundaries of what is "fearful" '. Tracing the adjective '*unheimlich*', he finds, surprisingly, that in one of its uses '*heimlich*', the ostensible antonym, is virtually a synonym. He quotes Grimm's dictionary to this effect: 'From the idea of "home-like", "belonging to the house", the further idea is developed of something withdrawn from the eyes of others, something concealed, secret . . . .' From this, Freud concludes that those things which give us a sense of the uncanny are those which recall repressed infantile fantasies, wishes, or modes of thought, those in general which remind us of primary psychic processes. Thus the coincidental granting of a wish is uncanny because it recalls the 'omnipotence of thoughts' which is believed in in childhood, and thus an epileptic seizure is an uncanny thing to witness because it arouses 'the feeling that automatic, mechanical processes are at work, concealed beneath the ordinary appearances of animation'. The distinction Freud makes between the uncanny and the fantastic is parallel to Kayser's distinction between true grotesque and the fairy tale – for example, according to Freud, the ghosts in Shakespeare do not seem uncanny because 'we order our judgment to the imaginary reality imposed on us by the writer, and regard souls, spirits and spectres as though their existence had the same validity in their world as our own has in the external world'; but 'the situation is altered as soon as the writer pretends to move in the world of common reality'.

We may note here (i) the link between Bergson's view of the comic (see section 32 below) and Freud's perception of the uncanniness of 'automatic, mechanical processes'; (ii) the potential for a very 'homely unhomeliness' or chummy terror or inoffensive offence which is built into the mechanism – but which will retain the disquieting energies of the 'primary psychic processes' none the less; (iii) the fact (which Steig de-emphasises) that Freud associates the roots of the uncanny with Oedipal anxieties and the threat of 'castration' (that difficult Freudian notion which relates all fears of separation-from and of disintegration to the puzzles of sexual identity that confront the young child).

Steig next cautions us that 'the uncanny and the grotesque should not be taken as identical'.

The grotesque involves the arousing of anxiety by giving expression to infantile fears, fantasies and impulses; what distinguishes it from the purely uncanny is that in the latter defenses against anxiety are weak, while in the grotesque the threatening material is distorted in the direction of harmlessness without completely attaining it. That is, the defense is still only partially successful, in that it allows some anxiety to remain, and characteristically will even contribute to the arousing of some anxiety. This is the basic paradox of the grotesque: it is double-edged, it at once allays and intensifies the effect of the uncanny; in pure comedy, at the other end of the spectrum from the uncanny, the defense is complete, and detachment is achieved. It is noteworthy in this regard that a psychoanalytic interpretation of the 'grotesque-comic sublimation' in neurotics (the ridiculing of others to alleviate a sense of personal worthlessness) suggests that this defense is unstable, and typically fails of the kind of total ego-mastery achieved by the comic, anxiety repeatedly breaking through.

Steig, 'Defining The Grotesque'.

(Shades of Basil Fawlty!)

6 THREAT/FUN

Steig concludes, via a contrast between two examples of the grotesque in Dickens (Mrs Clennam in *Little Dorrit* as a figure of threat and Mrs Gamp in *Martin Chuzzlewit* as a figure of fun), by dividing the grotesque into threatening and comic branches.

The peculiar attractiveness of Mrs Gamp recalls Ernst Kris's insistence that the comic is liberating, that it is a form of 'regression in the service of the ego', by means of which 'we can throw off the fetters of logical thought and revel in a long-forgotten freedom'. This statement will help us to modify our model of the grotesque, in which caricature and comedy have been seen up to now primarily as defenses against anxiety. To the extent that these techniques disguise the repressed material, they are defensive, but they also *allow for* the expression of this material, in part by virtue of their being in themselves a reflection of childhood impulses, but primarily through their function of allaying anxiety, and hence weakening inhibitions.

We may incorporate this concept in our final definition of the grotesque: The grotesque involves the manag-

Animation by Terry Gilliam for *Monty Python's Flying Circus*. BBC/Python (Monty) Pictures Ltd.

ing of the uncanny by the comic. More specifically: a) When the infantile material is primarily threatening, comic techniques, including caricature, diminish the threat through degradation or ridicule; but at the same time, they may also enhance anxiety through their aggressive implications and through the strangeness they lend to the threatening figure. b) In what is usually called the comic-grotesque, the comic in its various forms lessens the threat of identification with infantile drives by means of ridicule; at the same time, it lulls inhibitions and makes possible on a preconscious level the same identification that it appears to the conscience or superego to prevent. In short, both extreme types of the grotesque (and there are many instances in between) return us to childhood – the one attempts a liberation from fear, while the other attempts a liberation from inhibition; but in both a state of unresolved tension is the most common result, because of the intrapsychic conflicts involved.

Steig, op.cit.

7 NOTHING MORE?

Let us return to Alan Brien again, this time reviewing Terry Gilliam's first solo film, *Jabberwocky*.

If *Jabberwocky* . . . had surfaced at some off-beat cinema club, complete with subtitles and credits stuffed with names containing more xyz's than vowels, I would be the first to interpret it as a phantasmagoric parable foretelling the imminent decline and fall of Western civilisation . . . .

The Python humour . . . is notorious for being infantile hysterics inflated often to the level of genius, with a characteristic delight in dung, blood, insanity, mutilation, torture, freaks, indecent exposure and rude words and gestures. Much of it is intended to be nothing more than loony outrageousness . . . .But everything means something, and it can be no accident that *Jabberwocky* bears almost no relation to Lewis Carroll but turns out to be instead an uncannily persuasive Breughelesque portrait of the Middle Ages with many slyly snide sideglances at the modern day. For what distinguishes the Python approach from the *Helzapoppin*/Marx Brothers/Goodies style extravaganza is that it creates its comic-cartoon fantasy world with immense care for realistic, tangible detail, mixing together genuine beauty and real horror in a way that is sometimes reminiscent of Bergman or Fellini. Terry Bedford's photography would not have disgraced either . . . .

Sunday Times, 3 April 1977.

Generous though it finally is, this review reveals one of the problems with a 'return to childhood' theory of the grotesque, however true: it can look reductive. Once Brien has written 'infantile', a whole set of worries about 'grown-up cinema' vs. 'escapist cinema', foreign films vs. the home product (all too *heimlich*?), realism vs. fantasy is unleashed. That 'loony outrageousness' should *mean* anything is unthinkable – yet at the same time fascinating.

Time Bandits, as an explicitly child-oriented film, raises the problem even more sharply, as Margaret Hinxman's review in the *Daily Mail* demonstrates.

A deliciously imaginative adventure of let's pretend – or a severe case of arrested development? Your reaction to *Time Bandits* depends on how hooked or not you are on the Monty Python brand of scatty humour . . . [*Time Bandits* is] very much in line with the current trend of box-office hits – from *Superman II* and *Clash of the Titans* to the soon-to-be-released *Raiders of the Lost Ark* – that cater to the kid in all of us.

Daily Mail, 17 July 1981.

8 RUSKIN: THE IMAGINATION AT PLAY IS LIKE BAD CHILDREN

More on 'childishness': Steig praises the psychological penetration of John Ruskin's pre-Freudian view of the grotesque. (Coincidence: Robert Hewison, author of *Monty Python: The Case Against,* the study of the censorship struggles in which the Pythons have at various times been involved, is also a Ruskin expert.)

His initial premise, expressed in the 'Grotesque Renaissance' chapter of *The Stones of Venice,* is that there are two main kinds of grotesque, 'sportive' and 'terrible', which are composed, respectively, of 'ludicrous' and 'fearful' elements; but neither of these two kinds is often found in isolation – they are usually combined in some way. Rather than summarize the elaborate fourfold description of the grotesque that Ruskin here develops, it will be more convenient to make use of the later, threefold scheme in *Modern Painters,* part IV, chapter 8. There Ruskin lists three basic psychological processes from which grotesque art arises: 'healthful but irrational play of the imagination in times of rest'; 'irregular and accidental contemplation of terrible things; or evil in general'; and 'the confusion of the imagination by the presence of truths which it cannot wholly grasp'. But the succeeding paragraphs suggest that these distinctions are far from mutually exclusive, because 'the imagination, when at play, is curiously like bad children, and likes to play with fire', and thus 'it is hardly ever free from some slight taint of the inclination to evil; still more rarely is it, when so free, natural to the mind; for the moment we begin to contemplate sinless beauty we are apt to get serious; and moral fairy tales . . . are hardly ever . . . naturally imaginative . . . . The moment any real vitality enters them, they are nearly sure to . . . connect themselves with the evil-enjoying branch.' This seems a remarkable foreshadowing of the psychoanalytic view of the sources of artistic imagination, if we take Ruskin's 'evil' to be equivalent to the unconscious, or more specifically, the id. For while Ruskin wishes to believe that there is a kind of grotesque art that is healthy and free from evil, and another which is 'noble' and expresses otherwise inexpressible truths, he is at the same time aware that the grotesque usually involves itself with the forbidden. Although Ruskin's terms are almost invariably genetic, he never ties down the grotesque to particular conflicts in the author; he is trying rather to discover universal qualities, and terms like *ludicrous* and *fearful* refer as much to effect as to cause. And while Ruskin explicitly locates both evil and the inexpressible in the supernatural realm, this is not as crucial to his argument as it is to his religious position; for what emerges from his discussion is that the grotesque is an imaginative playing with the forbidden or the inexpressible (and perhaps that which is inexpressible is so because it is forbidden?).

Steig, op.cit.

9 PYTHON ADOLESCENCES

The possible roots of Python grotesquerie in its members' earliest childhoods are not part of the public record, but Python adolescences have not gone unexamined by interviewers, themselves (like the Pythons? like us all?) caught up in Popular Freudianism, nicely characterised by Richard Dyer (*Stars,* London, 1979, p. 138) as involving 'the notion of the Id, or that which is repressed, always threatening to burst forth and somehow, by its very force and intensity, being thought of as more "real" than the super-ego that controls it'.

So Michael Watts (*The Times,* 16 July 1981) gets this out of Terry Gilliam:

He admits to no style in his films, and says he has thoroughly eclectic tastes. What excites him are rich medieval images and gothic grotesquerie.

His animation can be uncommonly gruesome grand guignol: a persistent image is of a huge foot (actually, from Bronzino's Cupid) flattening a hapless victim. A reaction, he muses, to the stultifying perfection of his adolescent surroundings in California, where 'everything is based on beauty and health, and the abnormal, the ugly, the unpleasant are hidden away'.

Graham Chapman, in the later of his two interviews for *Gay News* (interviewer, Roger Baker), admits to an inferiority complex.

'What I do know is that I've always had a slight feeling of inferiority . . . . Going from an ordinary grammar school to Cambridge was difficult for me, and it was then I found I needed the booze. I was bad at taking criticism because I was bad at self-criticism. I was a timid little thing, and felt very protected by being a member of a group – the Monty Python team, I mean. If mistakes were made then the whole group took responsibility, you weren't on your own. Now I'm not as afraid as I was. I don't mind making my own mistakes and I'm more prepared to be mentally naked.'

Did he, I wondered, regard himself as a particularly armoured person? I reminded him that in the *Gay News* interview eight years ago, when talking about his openly gay lifestyle and how the neighbours reacted, he'd remarked, 'Mind you, I'm a well-known loonie, so it doesn't really matter'. So did he tend to look for things to hide behind – such as alcohol and being a loonie? The manic humour of the Monty Python kind, so often verging on hysteria, has sometimes struck me as a way of coping with horror too frightful to confront openly.

Graham smiles, nods. 'The first defence I took up was smoking a pipe – you can appear to be intelligent without saying anything. Now I do hide behind being eccentric.'

Gay News, no. 201, 1980.

John Cleese looks back on an over-sheltered youth, according to Hunter Davies.

He was an only child and was rather cosseted, protected and a trifle spoiled. 'I never had a bike. My parents thought I might hurt myself.' He in turn never thought of asking for one.

'John's birth was a bit of a bombshell', says Mrs Cleese. 'We'd been married 14 years – and there was a war on. I know he thinks we were a bit over-protective. He's told me enough times about the fact he never had a bike. But there was no need to have one. His school was opposite our house . . . .'

Tim Brooke-Taylor, who met Cleese at Cambridge: 'He was always very aware of having had a rather sheltered background. He never had a bike, did you know? Oh, he's told you that. When I met his parents I realised it was true. I remember his mother telling me to make sure he had a vest and a woolly jumper on. He was about 24 or 25 at the time. He made things worse by worrying them unduly. I remember being abroad with him when he wrote a postcard home to his mother saying he was going to take a ride on a new experimental monorail which was very safe, not to worry, it only did 250 miles an hour, though this was its maiden trip . . . '

Sunday Times, 6 March 1977.

An earlier Cleese profile by William Davis in the *Telegraph* suggests an anti-'system', anti-unexamined-values reaction on the young Cleese's part paralleling Gilliam's horror of 'beauty and health' – a reaction, *Telegraph* readers will have been glad to learn, which did not leave him 'a self-confident rebel'.

He went to public school, and thinks that a good deal of the Monty Python comedy comes from a reaction against the system. 'Looking back I see a whole set of values being imposed on me which I must have absorbed and not questioned for at least another three or four years.' He certainly questions them now – though he maintains that, far from being a self-confident rebel, he is ridden with self-doubt and very vulnerable.

Most of the other members of the team come from the same sort of strata, and their feelings were probably best expressed by the 'Twit of the Year Contest', another famous *Python* sketch. John played Nigel Nigel Hyphen Hyphen Stroke Money, 'a really excellent twit. Beat a boy to death at Eton for being middle class.' The sketch is very funny, but it is more than routine comedy performed by professionals prepared to behave foolishly for the sake of entertaining the public. It is pure satire, and it is all the more effective because of its underlying contempt.

Daily Telegraph, 21 June 1974.

10 'A TERROR OF BEING DEVOURED, TORN UP AND DESTROYED BY HER'

Now, for a moment, let us turn from Popular Freud to the real difficult thing.

The version of psychoanalytic thought which Steig uses suffers, it could be argued, from an overly 'functionalist' bias: that is, everything in the psyche either *works* (balancing this drive against that anxiety, say) or it doesn't – in the latter case we speak of neurosis, and try to cure it. The machinery is complicated and conflict-ridden, but at the end of the day it all *ought* to work.

In England Melanie Klein and in France Jacques Lacan preserved contact with the more tragic, more unaccommodatable side of Freud's thought. Klein's work with very young children revealed in the child a still inchoate, hence terrifying, landscape of anxieties about, first, the child's body and what the big people will do to it, and then, about what the child's own fearful, hostile wishes might do to the bodies of the big people. Lacan, in the course of his intricate, notoriously free-wheeling but immensely suggestive theoretical elaborations, absorbed these Kleinian discoveries into a wider semiotic framework: that is, the *meaning* of these earliest images and later evocations of them is to be sought, but only through the complex conflict-collaboration between their realm (the Imaginary) and the realm of inter-subjectively guaranteed codes (language, kinship: Lacan calls this the Symbolic).

Until someone attempts it, we can't be sure what a Kleinian or a Lacanian analysis of Python would look like. To anticipate this, here are a passage from Klein and two from Lacan developing Kleinian themes.

Klein ('Some Reflections on *The Oresteia*', in *Our Adult World and Other Essays*, London, 1963, reprinted in *Envy and Gratitude and Other Works*, London, 1975) describes the process of splitting (into 'good' and 'bad') that the infant performs in experiencing his or her first objects and people. In a first phase (the 'paranoid-schizoid position'), the child is riven by fears and corresponding destructive impulses which later (the 'depressive position' – perhaps the terminology is unduly frightening) he or she will try to make reparation for – in some cases, eventually, through creating art.

In the analysis of young children, I discovered a ruthless and persecuting super-ego, co-existing with the relation to the loved and even idealized parents. Retrospectively I found that during the first three months, in which destructive impulses, projection and splitting are at their height, frightening and persecuting figures are part of the infant's emotional life. To begin with they represent the frightening aspects of the mother and threaten the infant with all evils which he in states of hate and rage directs against his primal object. Although these figures are counteracted by love towards the mother, they are nevertheless the cause of great anxieties. From the beginning, introjection and projection are operative and are the basis for the internalization of the first and fundamental object, the mother's breast and the mother, both in her frightening and in her good aspects. It is this internalization which is the foundation of the super-ego. I tried to show that even the child who has a loving relation with his mother has also unconsciously a terror of being devoured, torn up and destroyed by her. These anxieties, though modified by a growing sense of reality, go on to a greater or lesser extent throughout early childhood.

Persecutory anxieties of this nature are part of the paranoid-schizoid position which characterizes the first few months of life. It includes a certain amount of schizoid withdrawal; also strong destructive impulses (the projection of which creates persecutory objects) and a splitting of the mother figure into a very bad part and an idealized good one. There are many other processes of splitting, such as fragmentation and a strong impetus to relegate the terrifying figures into the deep layers of the unconscious. Among the mechanisms at their height during this stage is the denial of all frightening situations; this is bound up with idealization. From the earliest stage onwards these processes are reinforced by repeated experience of frustration, which can never be completely avoided.

It is part of the young infant's anxiety situation that the terrifying figures cannot be completely split off. Moreover, projection of hate and destructive impulses can succeed only up to a point, and the division between the loved and the hated mother cannot be fully maintained. Therefore the infant is unable to escape altogether from feelings of guilt, though in the early stages these are only evanescent.

All these processes are bound up with the infant's drive towards symbol formation and form part of his phantasy life. Under the impact of anxiety, frustration and his insufficient ability to express his emotions towards his loved objects, he is driven to transfer his emotions and anxieties on to the objects by which he is surrounded. This transfer occurs first of all to parts of his own body as well as parts of his mother's body . . . .

I came in the course of my work to see more clearly that a corollary to the persecutory aspects of the internalized parents is their idealization. From the beginning, under the influence of the life instinct, the infant also introjects a good object, and the pressure of anxiety leads to the tendency to idealize this object. This has repercussions on the development of the super-ego. We are reminded here of Freud's view, expressed in his paper on 'Humour', that the kind attitude of the parents enters into the child's super-ego.

When persecutory anxiety is still in the ascendant, early feelings of guilt and depression are to some extent experienced as persecution. Gradually, with increasing strength of the ego, greater integration and progress in the relation to whole objects, persecutory anxiety loses in power and depressive anxiety dominates. Greater integration implies that hate in some measure becomes mitigated by love, that the capacity for love gains in strength, and that the split between hated and therefore terrifying objects, and loved ones, diminishes. Evanescent feelings of guilt, linked with a feeling of incapacity to prevent destructive impulses from harming the loved objects, increase and become more poignant. I have described this stage as the depressive position, and my psycho-analytic experience with children and adults has confirmed my findings that to go through the depressive position results in very painful feelings . . . .

Klein, 'Some Reflections on *The Oresteia*' (1963).

Lacan ('Aggressivity in Psychoanalysis' (1948), in *Ecrits: A Selection,* tr. Alan Sheridan, London, 1977) invokes one of Terry Gilliam's favourite artists, Bosch, as providing 'an atlas of all the aggressive images that torment mankind', images originating in the earliest anxieties of the child about the integrity of his or her own body. (In the excerpt which follows, the translation has been modified in places.)

After the repeated failures of classical psychology to account for the mental phenomena known as images . . . , psychoanalysis made the first successful attempt to operate at the level of the concrete reality that they represent. This was because it set out from their formative function in the subject, demonstrating that where everyday images determine certain individual inflections of tendencies, they do so as variations of the matrices constituted for the 'instincts' themselves by those other specific factors which we call by the antique term *imago.*

Among these *imagos* are some that represent the preferred vectors of aggressive intentions, which they provide with an efficacy that might be called magical. These are the images of castration, mutilation, dismemberment, dislocation, evisceration, devouring, bursting open of the body, in short, the *imagos* that I have grouped together under the heading – which indeed seems a structural one – of *imagos of the fragmented body*.

There is a specific relation here between man and his own body that is manifested in a series of social practices – from rites involving tattooing, incision, and circumcision in primitive societies to what, in advanced societies, might be called the Procrustean arbitrariness of fashion, in that it denies respect (itself a fairly recent cultural development) for the natural forms of the human body.

One only has to listen to children aged between two and five playing, alone or together, to know that the pulling off of the head and the ripping open of the belly are themes that occur spontaneously in their imagination, and that this is corroborated by the experience of the doll torn to pieces.

We must turn to the works of Hieronymus Bosch for an atlas of all the aggressive images that torment mankind. The prevalence that psychoanalysis has discovered among them of images of a primitive autoscopy of the oral and cloacal organs has engendered the forms of demons. These are to be found even in the narrow archway of the *angustiae* of birth depicted in the gates of the abyss through which they thrust the damned, and even in the narcissistic structures of those glass spheres in which the exhausted partners of the garden of delights are held captive.

Lacan has laid great stress on the moment when the child first recognises himself or herself in a mirror: the lack of physical co-ordination that the infant has painfully experienced ('natal prematuration': we seem to be born, unlike calves or colts, before we are physiologically very 'together') is 'repaired' in the wholeness of the image. This grasp of an image of oneself via the mirror, and the correlative separation-out of images of important adult figures and siblings as wholly distinct from oneself, is at once a triumphant and a fraught achievement. The dominating images of one's later life will always be inflected by one's particular experience of this moment.

What I have called the *mirror stage* is interesting in that it manifests the affective dynamism by which the subject originally identifies himself with the visual *Gestalt* of his own body: in relation to the still very profound lack of co-ordination of his own motility, it represents an ideal unity, a salutary *imago*; it is invested with all the original distress resulting from the child's intra-organic and relational discordance during the first six months, when he bears the signs, neurological and humoral, of a physiological natal prematuration . . . .

Only Melanie Klein, working on the child at the very limit of the appearance of language, dared to project subjective experience back to that earlier period when observation enables us nevertheless to affirm its dimension, in the simple fact for example that a child who does not speak reacts differently to punishment or to brutality.

Through her we know the function of the imaginary primordial enclosure formed by the *imago* of the mother's body; through her we have the cartography, drawn by the children's own hands, of the mother's internal empire, the historical atlas of the intestinal divisions where the *imagos* of the father and brothers (real or virtual) and the voracious aggression of the subject himself dispute their deleterious dominance over her sacred regions. We know, too, the persistence in the subject of this shadow of the *bad internal objects,* linked with some accidental *association* (to use a term that we should accept in the organic sense that it assumes in our experience, as opposed to the abstract sense that it retains in Humean ideology). Hence we can understand by what structural means the re-evocation of certain imaginary *personae,* the reproduction of certain situational inferiorities, may *disconcert* in the most strictly predictable way the adult's voluntary functions: namely, their fragmenting effect on the *imago* of the original identification.

Lacan, 'Aggressivity in psychoanalysis' (1948).

11 CLEESE'S BODY: VISUAL GESTALT OF

The surprising thing about Cleese is not that he is so funny, but that he is funny in so many different ways . . . . His lanky, almost anonymous figure has an amazing flexibility: in repose he gives an impression of old-fashioned grace, a Royal Flying Corps type. Then

Fawlty Towers. BBC copyright.

the frenzy descends and he is gallows-humour incarnate, second cousin to Dürer's skeletal horseman carrying the plague, all bony elbows and knees, ghastly grin and hollow eye-sockets. It is this unnerving mixture of violence and urbanity that distinguished his best Monty Python characters and made Basil Fawlty a unique exhibit in the comedy chamber of horrors.

– Lee Langley, *Guardian,* 19 December 1975: the headline-writer here came up with one of the more haunting plays on the Python name by entitling Langley's article 'Monty's Double'.

12 NOSE AND BREAST, PUPPET AND CORPSE

The psychoanalytic perspective makes grotesque art look no less grotesque: here, accusations of reductionism seem inappropriate. If anything, reading the following passage from Philip Thomson's very useful little book in the 'Critical Idiom' series *The Grotesque* (London, 1972) with a Kleinian eye enhances the monstrosity of the extract from Sterne he quotes.

The difference between the bizarre and the grotesque is mainly one of degree. The grotesque is more radical and usually more aggressive. Kayser expresses the difference by calling the grotesque more dangerous: the bizarre, he points out, can be used synonymously with 'very strange', 'outlandish' – it lacks the disturbing quality of the grotesque . . . . Of course, the dividing line may in any case be very difficult to draw, and one can point to a number of works where the bizarre turns into the grotesque for a brief moment. We can describe this process in technical terms in the following way: something which is very strange, and perhaps ludicrous as well, is made so exceedingly abnormal that our laughter at the ludicrous and eccentric is intruded on by feelings of horror or disgust; or, a scene or character which is laughably eccentric suddenly becomes problematic, and our reaction to it mixed, through the appearance of something quite at odds with the comic. We may observe this phenomenon in an example from *Tristram Shandy*:

> That this *Ambrose Paroeus* was chief surgeon and nose-mender to *Francis* the ninth of *France,* and in high credit with him and the two preceding, or succeeding kings (I know not which) – and that, except in the slip he made in his story of *Taliacotius's* noses, and his manner of setting them on – he was esteemed by the whole college of physicians at that time, as more knowing in matters of noses, than anyone who had ever taken them in hand.

Now *Ambrose Paroeus* convinced my father, that the true and efficient cause of what had engaged so much the attention of the world, and upon which *Prignitz* and *Scroderus* had wasted so much learning and fine parts – was neither this nor that – but that the length and goodness of the nose was owing simply to the softness and flaccidity in the nurse's breast – as the flatness and shortness of *puisne* noses was to the firmness and elastic repulsion of the same organ of nutrition in the hale and lively – which, tho' happy for the woman, was the undoing of the child, inasmuch as his nose was so snubb'd, so rebuff'd, so rebated, and so refrigerated thereby, as never to arrive *ad mensuram suam legitimam,* – but that in case of the flaccidity and softness of the nurse or mother's breast – by sinking into it, quoth *Paroeus,* as into so much butter, the nose was comforted, nourish'd, plump'd up, refresh'd, refocillated, and set a growing for ever.

I have but two things to observe of Paroeus; first, That he proves and explains all this with the utmost chastity and decorum of expression – for which may his soul for ever rest in peace! . . .

(Everyman edition, London, 1956, pp. 169-70)

What begins as a merely eccentric and bizarre account of a theory of nose shapes and sizes becomes perhaps somewhat disturbing with the mention of the infant nose sinking into the breast 'as into so much butter'. It would be too much to say that this image is monstrous, but there is something unsettling about the confusion between animate and inanimate, between the female breast and a lump of butter (perhaps the association of butter with milk, in the context, adds to this), and about the suggestion that the nose actually feeds upon the breast. But the feeling is there only for a moment; instead of developing the image further in the direction of grotesquery, as he doubtless could have, Sterne – and this is typical of him – returns to his whimsical style, with assurances that Paroeus expounds his theory 'with the utmost chastity and decorum of expression'. . . .

The confusion between animate and inanimate referred to above recalls an important feature of the original grotesque paintings described by Vitruvius and imitated by Renaissance painters: the interweaving of plant, animal, human and architectural forms, so that a stone pedestal would become the torso of a human figure with curling plants for arms and an animal's head. It also brings to mind those theories of the comic, principally Henri Bergson's in *Le rire,* which attempt to locate the source of laughter in the perception of living things, especially human beings, as inanimate, and conversely also in the perception of inanimate objects as alive. Bergson's is a rather narrow and one-sided definition of the comic, and Kayser is closer to the mark when he classes this kind of confusion as one of the basic *grotesque* techniques, and mentions in this connection the puppet or marionette. Certainly there is something potentially grotesque about marionettes, automatons and the like. Human-like, animated yet actually lifeless objects, they are apt to be simultaneously comical and eerie – comical because of their imperfect approximation to human form and behaviour, eerie probably because of age-old, deep-rooted fears in man of animated and human-like objects. Conversely, a human being giving the appearance of being a marionette or robot is likewise grotesque: comical and strangely disturbing at the same time. Hence also the common description of dead bodies: 'The body lay in a grotesque position' – i.e. in a position normally only assumable by marionettes and dolls, with limbs and head in unnatural positions.

Thomson, *The Grotesque.*

13 RIGOR MORTIS IN THE SERVICE LIFTS

On the subject of dead bodies: here is Alex Hamilton talking to John Cleese during the writing of the second series of *Fawlty Towers.*

In Falmouth, I recalled, a hotelier told me his great problem was estimating how many at breakfast. In high season his guests pegged out on him in droves. It occurred to me there was a feature in this.

'You alarm me' [said Cleese]. 'I shall now point to one of our episodes called "Corpse". My friend at Langan's, who trained at the Savoy, told me without a moment's thought that the worst problem was the dead bodies. People, as you say, pegging out inconveniently. The Savoy gets 10 or 12 a year. Naturally they don't want to disturb the surviving guests' breakfasts by taking corpses through the dining room. Terrible problems of rigor mortis they have in the service lifts. It makes a wonderful episode.'

Guardian, 10 January 1979.

14 BECAUSE WE ALL HAVE MOTHERS

In her review of *Time Bandits* Virginia Dignam complained:

This male-written, male-orientated look at history has only two female parts . . . . There is also a cameo role of Kevin's mum, a woman obsessed with electronic gadgetry and so inept she has to consult the picture on the packet of pre-cooked junk food in order to find out which is the chicken . . . . Women don't come out of *Time Bandits* too well, the only historical characters worth visiting being exclusively male. What about Nell Gwynne, Elizabeth I, or Queen Victoria even?

Morning Star, 17 July 1981.

(Actually, John Cleese has played Elizabeth I: see section 35 below.) And Paul Gambaccini, writing in *Rolling Stone* for an American audience, has to get Graham Chapman to explain the Pythons' fondness for drag.

At Cambridge, the Pythons first tried what, for Americans, is a characteristic oddity of their humor. 'There were no women actors at Cambridge', Chapman explains, 'and the women we wrote were certainly not meant to be attractive, so there was no reason to actually have real breasts. We might as well do them.' Do them they did. Indeed, several Pythons may perform a cinema first in *Brian* when they appear in double drag: only men are allowed to participate in the stoning, so the 'women' are forced to put on beards and other camouflage.

Rolling Stone, 18 October 1979.

A striking passage in Graham Chapman's first *Gay News* interview, taking off from the question of the women's movement, should perhaps be read with caution: the interview occasion seems to have been an especially convivial one (on this, see the introduction to the second interview). The interviewer is Richard Adams.

. . . Women are very, very oppressed. They are certainly not equal human beings at the moment, and that is *very* unfortunate. It's particularly unfortunate for us, because we all have mothers, and our mothers, in the position of being oppressed, in turn oppress us, push us with all kinds of views we shouldn't really hold. In fact, I think mothers as such, as produced by our society, are probably responsible for most of the wars we've ever had. Because they teach us to be so butch, they teach us to be aggressive towards little Johnnie next door – it starts right from the cradle and goes on forever to the extent that we eventually go to war against another nation . . . .

Maybe . . . you shouldn't treat children as being different sexes at all. I think that's the ideal situation, actually, because children aren't different sexes, and neither, for that matter, are adults. In my experience, going to bed with a man and going to bed with a woman is totally similar – absolutely totally similar.

But do you enjoy them equally, in retrospect?

No – obviously I prefer men. I *did* enjoy women a great deal, but then I found, partly because of their . . . the way they want you to live, which on the whole is a kind of middle-class way to live . . . that I couldn't live with that. And anyway, I don't quite know why, but I prefer men physically. I've no answer to that. I don't know why. But I do. But a woman, because of the way she's taught in her early life, is very conservative. Maybe this is something innate, because the woman on the whole is the person who brings up the family, and she is therefore more conservative. On the whole women are conservative in every way, politically too . . . .

This is unkind, isn't it.

Is that what you reject?

. . . women's conditioning? Entirely. I'm very pro-women's lib, I really am, 'cos that would be homosexual liberation as well, it really would. 'Let my son do what he wants.'

Gay News, no.4, 1972.

The accusation woman = parent = stuffy/anti-freedom/oppressive (under present conditions) should be compared with a passage in Anne Thompson's interview with Terry Gilliam in *Film Comment,* where Kevin's parents' awfulness in *Time Bandits* gets defined in national rather than in sexual terms.

Do you think you're doing something along the lines of what [George] Lucas is doing, which is bringing back some of the mythology that's been lost to children?

Yes, I think there's something awful with being an American. You're stuck with it. I live out of the country, and I make films out of the country; but I actually do

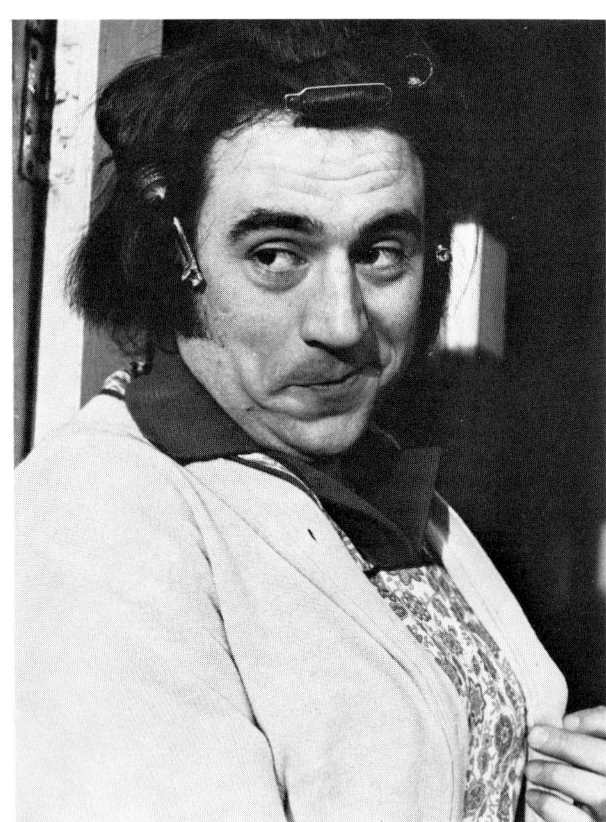

Terry Jones in *Monty Python's Flying Circus.* BBC copyright.

think I'd like to have some effect on the country. I'm well aware of what I'm doing and having Evil being obsessed with technology is very important to me. It's a very dangerous thing, and it isn't the answer to everything, and that's why we've got the Supreme Being obsessed with woolly-minded thinking and rainbows – really nice things. God is British, and Evil is American. There's no question about it.

Are British children better off?

I think so. They have less, so it gives them a chance to contribute more.

Do they read more?

Yes, I think they're more literate. England is a richer base of fantasy, intellectual curiosity, individualism. I'm always amazed at America, a country that always prided itself on its individuals. It's the least individual-based country I've ever been in, almost. They talk about it all the time, but people basically do things in mobs. You have to hunt for individuals in America. In England, what's always wonderful is that people, like accountants and little bureaucrats – people you'd think wouldn't have a weird thought in their mind at all – they live much richer lives. They protect their own personal space and flourish in that.

So the British parents that you paint such a vivid picture of are American parents?

No, they're definitely British. They're the New Britain, which really horrifies me, parents like that who are obsessed with Americans. When America does something, it does it rather spectacularly. England does it on a rather nasty, tacky little level.

Film Comment, November/December 1981.

15 BACK TO THE NOSE

Thomson (cf. above, section 12) is concerned to establish the point at which caricature passes over into the grotesque.

The grotesque has always been strongly associated with caricature, and even placed in the same category by some theorists, notably those who saw simple distortion as the basic principle in grotesque art. Caricature may be briefly defined as the ludicrous exaggeration of characteristic or peculiar features. A major distinction from the grotesque as we have sought to describe it at once becomes clear: in caricature there need be no suggestion of the *confusion* of heterogeneous and incompatible elements, no sense of the intrusion of alien elements. The difference can be felt plainly in one's reaction. One laughs at a caricature because a recognizable or typical person or characteristic is distorted (or stylized) in a ridiculous and amusing way – that is, a peculiar feature is exaggerated to the point of abnormality. It is a straightforward, uncomplicated reaction to something which has a straightforward function and clearly discernible intention, whereas one's reaction to the grotesque is essentially divided and problematic. It only becomes difficult to distinguish between caricature and the grotesque . . . when the caricaturistic exaggeration becomes extreme or develops into exaggeration for its own sake. Thus a sketch of the late General de Gaulle in which the nose is made disproportionately large would be a caricature; but if one increasingly exaggerates the size of the nose until the point is reached where it appears that the rest of the face is entirely subservient to and controlled by the nose (the tail wagging the dog, as it were), then this is likely to be a grotesque caricature. Not only has the normal relationship of face to nose been reversed but the nose has taken on an almost autonomous quality and so to speak assumed a separate existence. In other words there is a norm for caricaturistic exaggeration – a norm of abnormality. When this norm is exceeded, the caricature is no longer simply funny, but disgusting or fearsome besides, for it approaches the realm of the monstrous. Many of the caricatures of Daumier, Grandville or of George Grosz are of this kind.

> The caricature which becomes abnormally abnormal, hence monstrous, may be compared to another example of the grotesque: the face you distort to amuse, then terrify, a child.

It should be clear that . . . the classic reaction to the grotesque – the experience of amusement and disgust, laughter and horror, mirth and revulsion, simultaneously, is partly at least a reaction to the highly *abnormal.* For the abnormal may be funny (this is accurately reflected in the every-day usage of 'funny' to mean both 'amusing' and 'strange') and on the other hand it may be fearsome or disgusting. Delight in novelty and amusement at a

No. 98. Horror.

Illustration from *A History of Caricature and Grotesque* by Thomas Wright, London, 1865.

divergence from the normal turns to fear of the unfamiliar and the unknown once a certain degree of abnormality is reached. Mirth at something which fails to conform to accepted standards and norms gives way to fear (and anger) when these norms are seen to be seriously threatened or attacked. This is a paradoxical matter, and we can perhaps make it clearer by taking the example of very small children (good guinea-pigs because their reactions are still spontaneous and uncomplicated) to whom one makes grimaces which increasingly distort the face. The child will laugh at the face pulled only up to a certain point (presumably, while it is still sure of the face as a familiar thing); once this point is passed, once the face becomes so distorted that the child feels threatened, it cries in fear. It is the thin dividing line between the two reactions which is of interest to the student of the grotesque, or, to put it more precisely, the situation where both reactions are evoked at the same time, where both the comic aspect of the abnormal and the fearful or disgusting aspect are felt equally . . . .

A further example may help to clarify what has been said about abnormality as an essential ingredient of the grotesque. In Smollett's *Humphry Clinker,* we are told of a 'famous Dr L – n' who, upon hearing complaints of the stench caused by river mud, launches 'into a learned investigation of the nature of stink'.

> He observed, that stink, or stench, meant no more than a strong impression on the olfactory nerves; and might be applied to substances of the most opposite qualities; that in the Dutch language, stinken signifies the most agreeable perfume, as well as the most fetid odour, . . . that the French were pleased with the putrid effluvia of animal food; and so were the Hottentots in Africa, and the Savages in Greenland; and that the Negroes on the coast of Senegal would not touch fish till it was rotten; strong presumptions in favour of what is generally called stink, as those nations are in a state of nature undebauched by luxury, unseduced by whim and caprice: that he had reason to believe the stercoraceous flavour, condemned by prejudice as a stink, was, in fact, most agreeable to the organs of smelling: for, that every person who pretended to nauseate the smell of another's excretions, snuffed up his own with particular complacency; for the truth of which he appealed to all the ladies and gentlemen then present: he said, the inhabitants of Madrid and Edinburgh found particular

satisfaction in breathing their own atmosphere, which was always impregnated with stercoraceous effluvia: that the learned Dr B–, in his treatise on the Four Digestions, explains in what manner the volatile effluvia from the intestines stimulate and promote the operations of the animal economy; he affirmed, the last Grand Duke of Tuscany, of the Medicis family, who refined upon sensuality with the spirit of a philosopher, was so delighted with that odour that he caused the essence of ordure to be extracted, and used it as the most delicious perfume: that he himself (the doctor) when he happened to be low-spirited, or fatigued with business, found immediate relief and uncommon satisfaction from hanging over the stale contents of a close-stool, while his servant stirred it about under his nose . . . .

(Penguin, 1967, pp. 45-6)

We may well call this passage extravagant, outlandish and indecent (all epithets commonly used in relation to the grotesque) but, as suggested earlier, we shall understand better the special quality of it and similar passages if we work with the more objective term 'abnormal'. The preposterous doctor and his eccentric ideas are so divergent from the norm that they excite both our laughter and our disgust.

Thomson, op.cit.

16 AN ASTONISHINGLY DIRTY PERIOD

There is, it seems, a certain scatological streak in [Gilliam's] outlook. He sees the Middle Ages . . . as an astonishingly dirty period, with people much the same as today, except that they have to wade through mire, animal ordure, and mountains of frightful garbage, and even the king has to pick bits of the palace ceiling out of his dinner before he can eat it. They shot their street scenes on the *Oliver* set at Shepperton during the heat of last summer. 'This film looks so vivid', said someone at a preview, 'you can *smell* the Middle Ages' . . .

'The thing about all this nonsense', says Terry Gilliam, 'is that it's based on real believable situations and people. I've tried to make it look real – their hair is greasy, their clothes are ragged, the dirt is all there. Some people are already taking it seriously, and seeing in the picture socio-economic-religious pretensions. Could it be that the reviews, particularly in France, might be funnier than the film?'

– George Perry, *Sunday Times,* 27 March 1977. Or, as Alexander Walker put it in the *Evening Standard,* 31 March 1977: 'Director Terry Gilliam applies neo-realism to the Middle Ages and comes up with a comedy that looks like a dirtied-up Bruegel or a goonish Bosch.'

17 FAR FROM PERFECT AND GENTLE

Why does the Middle Ages mean so much to the Pythons? Terry Jones has made the most unexpected of their forays into that particular past.

[*Chaucer's Knight*] is a book that has been ticking over in the mind of Terry Jones for a decade, and may well revolutionise the state of Chaucerian scholarship. It is not quite as far from the Python clowning as it sounds.

'I suppose I was interested at school. You could see Chaucer was such a funny guy, and I've always liked jokes, and I was looking for jokes; but there were vast areas I couldn't understand; the Knight and the Knight's Tale, for example, didn't seem to make sense. You could see the same form happening as with the description of the Prioress – she could speak French very well, after the fashion of Stratford-atte-Bowe – but does Chaucer knock down the Knight in the same way?'

The youthful Jones pondered on this, and at Oxford he moved from literary critics to historians in an attempt to see what the lines would have meant to Chaucer's contemporaries. The Knight, he decided, was far from perfect and gentle . . . .

Unlike today's academics who merely record the date of the event, Chaucer's readers would have picked up the reference [to the Knight's having fought as a mercenary at Alexandria]; our saintly Crusading Knight is clearly a cross between a Callan, the lunatic mercenary of abortive Angolan fame, and a Belsen guard . . . .

It is for Terry Jones a labour of love. The study at the top of his house has become a Chaucer library with books whose total value must run into thousands of pounds, and clearly the scholarly work will not recoup this. He has not yet even a publisher.

'Compared with the original Chaucer, my book is elephantine. You're not going to get many laughs out of trying to explain 600-year-old jokes. I had hoped to write it in a non-academic style and get away from the terrible jargon of the *Chaucer Review*; I don't see why an academic book shouldn't be accessible to ordinary people, and it may get people to read Chaucer with more confidence. I feel that if you're going to read Chaucer, this is the kind of book you're going to have to read.' The academic world, of course, may like to respond with one of those gigantic Python boots that clump down from a great height and trample him into the dust.

Thus was Jones's *Chaucer's Knight* introduced (30 April 1977) to *Guardian* readers by Jonathan Sale three years before it was published. The world of scholarship is cut off from the people, stultifying (the subhead half-way through the article reads ' "Academic scholarship in this field shows an enormous ignorance" ') and threatening (the foot). The reader is meant to admire Jones's courage in taking it on as an outsider, but also to wonder at his quixotic, driven need to amass a library his book won't even pay for.

No. 63. A Feat of Arms.

Illustration from *A History of Caricature and Grotesque.*

18 'VOLE' AND REAL ALE, BUT SO MANY BOOKS

The Jones library makes an impression on other journalists. Here is Charles Spenser in the *New Standard* summing up the man.

The walls of [Jones's] room may be covered with *Life of Brian* posters but the book shelves are crammed with scholarly work on Chaucer. One of the books is by Jones himself . . . .

Despite the occasional flights into comic voices, there is no mistaking Jones's basic seriousness. A tall, warm man who is happily married with two young children he clearly dotes on, he speaks passionately about the follies of nuclear power and financed the founding of the environmental magazine *Vole.*

Searching for the good life, he even bought his own real ale brewery. On good days, he says, the beer is terrific.

New Standard, 28 November 1980.

A more inward look at Jones's interests was attempted by Alex Hamilton in the *Guardian.*

In the study of his home in Camberwell, a great critical apparatus of research tools has overpowered his shelves, with the single end of hammering at his obsession . . . .

From grammar school at Guildford, he had been interested in modern poetry and the Leavisite disciplines. Instead he found himself at Oxford, soaked in medieval studies.

But as a small child he had hated books about other children. He preferred tales of animals that lived in holes, or under roots, the infants' equivalent to science fiction. And the medieval world chimed with this, complete and watertight, intelligible in a way that the confusing modern world never is . . . .

Yet Hamilton goes on to reveal a Jones who admires Chaucer for reflecting the violence of his time, for being in touch with the plight of the common people and indeed addressing them. What kind of 'equivalent to science fiction' is such a Chaucer supposed to be for Jones?

It was the time of the Peasants' Revolt. Chaucer, the dominating figure of the age, was writing about the effects of war on the civilian population, not so much the death on the battlefield, but the stable blackened with smoke, a corpse in a bush with his throat cut, a man in bed with a stake driven through his throat. Furthermore, he was writing in English, dangerously open to the charge of providing wisdom for the common people. Why he did this is another pursuit [Jones would] like to take up.

Guardian, 18 January 1980.

19 VIOLENCE, RELIGION, AND THE SHAPE OF CHAUCER'S JOKES

The following passages are from Terry Jones's *Chaucer's Knight* (London, 1980).

[Chaucer] was outspoken against wars in which the innocent suffered . . . . Most significantly, as his own *Tale,* he chose to translate an uncompromising pacifist tract. Critics have, in the past, tended to minimize Chaucer's anti-war statements, dismissing them as either 'wholly conventional' or unoriginal. But they overlook the political climate in which Chaucer was writing, which would have given tremendous impact to any statement on the subject that he made. The peace with France was, of course, one of the major political controversies of the day. The 'hawks' versus 'doves' confrontation in Richard II's Court was no less dramatic than it was in this century in President Johnson's or President Nixon's Senate during the Vietnam War . . . . And yet in such an atmosphere Chaucer was bold enough to present *as his own personal statement* a pacifist tract – and a French one at that – opposing all wars . . . .

In any case, is it not manifestly an absurd idea to seek to prove religious truth by a contest of arms? It certainly seemed so to some of Chaucer's contemporaries. Christine de Pisan [in *The Book of Fayttes of Armes and of Chyvalrye,* trans. Caxton] regarded it as blasphemous:

> . . . to ask a thing against nature or above nature is a presumption and is displeasing to God, and to believe that the feeble shall overcome the strong, or the old the young, or the sick the healthy because of the justness of their cause . . . is but tempting God. And I say, for certain, if it happens that they should win it is but chance and not because they are in the right.

On that often quoted occasion in 1390, when the Saracens challenged the Christians to a tournament during the seige of Mahdia, there was, in fact, a considerable difference of opinion among the Christians as to whether or not they should accept it. The Lord of Coucy said that where the Christian faith was called into question, it was too serious a matter to be answered by one knight and that, 'such defyaunce in armes for suche a quarell ought nat to passe without great deliberation of good counsayle'.

In *Monty Python's Flying Circus,* the TV show in which I have been involved over the last ten years, we once did a sketch in which, instead of debating the existence or non-existence of God, a bishop and a humanist philosopher fought each other for it. It seems to me that Chaucer made this same joke almost six hundred years ago.

In his day, however, it had even more relevance, since he was in effect commenting on the Church's double-think on the subject of war. For the same Church that condemned tournaments, condoned and encouraged crusades in which, instead of two men, two nations fought each other to the death to prove the superiority of one religion over another . . . .

Once again this whole passage has followed the classic Chaucerian joke form. He first raised a balloon of expectation by telling us that the Knight had 'foughten for oure feith'. He then showed us the pin, when he told us that it was 'at Tramyssene'. He then applied the pin to the balloon by telling us it was 'In lystes thries' and the whole thing will burst in our faces in the next half line, when he cheerfully adds: 'and ay slayn his foo'.

(Jones's argument has been that to fight 'in the lists', i.e. in tournaments, would have deflated the reader's expectations of crusading, and that always to slay your foe under tournament conditions would have seemed more barbarous than skilful.)

20 THE PYTHON LITERARY GUILD

A word is in order about the Python books. Each member of the team has a book or books to his credit independently of strictly Python projects. And of course the Python books proper have been immensely popular. In 'Ten Years of Silly Publishing', Geoffrey Strachan of Methuen describes the phenomenon.

When we in Methuen started working with the six creators of *Monty Python's Flying Circus* one of the many things we learned from them quite quickly was the positive value they attached to the word 'silly'. Coming from a long tradition of explosive nonsense humour, echoing in their style elements of Rabelais, Carroll, Lear, the Marx Brothers and the Goons – as well as the clowning element that was already prevalent in student revue in the early '60s alongside the social satire – the Pythons made silly jokes and celebrated silliness in their writing. The Silly Party and the Extremely Silly Party and the Ministry of Silly Walks are amongst their most cherished creations.

At the end of the '60s we were seeking out humorous writers from other media who could write good funny books (just as *Punch* writers like A. P. Herbert and Sellar and Yeatman had done in the '20s and '30s). In March 1971 the *Monty Python* team agreed to write what was in early discussions referred to as *Monty Python's Big Book*. It was partly inspired by the style of large-format children's colour-illustrated books, partly by that of comic annuals. This was unusual in those days. But our working title, though slightly silly, wasn't silly enough. And so it became *Monty Python's Big Red Book* (after Chairman Mao's opus and the then recently published and highly controversial *Little Red School Book*). It was naturally decided that the cover should be blue (to the confusion of many people including one of our packers who, when finished copies arrived, telephoned the production department in panic, convinced that there was an error).

Because of the Pythons' concern about the detailed visual effect of every page, they quickly incorporated Derek Birdsall, as designer, into their team to work alongside Eric Idle, the editor. All text copy was shown to us (and it arrived over several weeks in a dazzling and confusing stream of odd bits of paper) but the Pythons had agreed that the only way to ensure the book looked how they wanted was to deliver it as 70 complete pages of camera-ready artwork . . . .

The Pythons, new to the world of books, learned fast: soon it was they who were teaching us the right approach to silly publishing. Hence the full page advertisement in *The Bookseller* on 10th July that began:

THE FORD MOTOR COMPANY
recommends
MONTY PYTHON'S BIG RED BOOK . . .

the first of a series of lies identified as such in a footnote.

Meanwhile, our sales representatives had been bemused to receive a memo part of which read as follows:

To: General Representatives
From: Col. 'Muriel' Volestrangler

I would like to apologise for the extremely sensible tone of the memo from Michael Turner. As you probably know, ordinary decent good honest behaviour is utterly foreign to the despicable group of people who masquerade under the cowardly pseudonym of Monty Python. I feel you should know that their Big Red Book is extremely tatty and full of very silly, stupid and childish features. Half of the pages are yellow, many of them are pink, a few pages are actually printed on cheap newsprint and some have even got holes in! . . .

I apologise for taking up your time like this, but I urge you not to fall for this glib claptrap from Methuen. Have nothing to do with this silly book. Shun it, do not buy it, above all, do not read it. I would thoroughly recommend that you sell *Harry's*

Bee instead, as Dostoievsky has always been my favourite writer.
Yours sincerely,
Col. 'Muriel' Volestrangler (Mrs)

. . . On 1st November the queue formed outside Blackwells half an hour before opening time . . . . The following autumn the same-size paperback edition sold 140,000 copies (and the two editions have now sold nearly 450,000). The Pythons, as usual, knew exactly how we should present the paperback, and the silly and mendacious 'special new hard-back edition' flash for the front cover was designed. When we expressed anxiety over the confusion this might cause to booksellers the Pythons stood firm. I had communicated the worry our marketing director had expressed to me in a cable from Australia:

PYTHON PLEASE REPEAT PLEASE DON'T CONFUSE THE BOOK TRADE BUT THINK UP SOME BRILLIANT ALTERNATIVE.

In reply Eric Idle wrote to me:

We've got the usual competition between salesmanship and a joke, and I think in this case that as the cover is not part of the advertising but part of the content of the book then we should be allowed to make this joke, and the stupidity potential of your booksellers should be overcome in some other manner. You could easily get printed a series of warnings for them that 'THIS IS A JOKE'. Provided they can read of course. As to our readers; as you've managed to flog them 80,000 copies of a red book that is blue don't you think they might just notice that what they are holding isn't a hardback at all?

We quickly saw the light: and over the years the Pythons continued to show that with their books there was in fact no conflict between salesmanship and a joke. When it came to the *Brand New Monty Python Bok* in 1973 none of us questioned the jacket and cover designs. The cover featured the appalling and misleading title: *Tits 'n Bums: A Weekly Look at Church Architecture,* suitably illustrated. This was chastely hidden under a stark black-and-white jacket adorned only with the faint but unmistakable blemish of greyish-brown fingerprints. In the first version of this design they were black and too obviously a fake: Terry Gilliam didn't want that – he wanted genuine confusion. The confusion arrived by telephone as soon as pre-publication orders began to be delivered ('I ordered 40 copies of this book and every single jacket is dirty. I want 40 replacement jackets'. 'The jacket is dirty so I think I'll just have to display it in the window without the jacket . . . Oh!'). Some people hated it again but the sales rolled in.

. . . You don't have to look far in the pages of any of the Python books to realise that they got the measure of the book trade early on. And if Book Club Associates in the summer of 1971 took offence at the 'Python Literary Guild's' introductory offer of 'one free tub of dung (plus monthly one dead Indian, tick if required)' they, like the rest of us, have learned to see the world through Python eyes since then . . . .

The Bookseller, 10 October 1981.

21 BAGEHOT: 'HOW CAN A SOUL BE A MERCHANT?'

From *Tits 'n Bums: A Weekly Look at Church Architecture* to some aspects of *Life of Brian* is clearly no great step; let us take it in the company of Walter Bagehot, eminent nineteenth-century theorist of British parliamentary institutions, and G. W. F. Hegel, the well-known philosopher. Our guide is Arthur Clayborough (*The Grotesque in English Literature*, Oxford, 1965).

With the view of Hegel and Ruskin that the grotesque in art is produced by the conflict between man's intuitions of the infinite and his physical limitations, we may compare a striking passage by Walter Bagehot:

> But taken as a whole, the universe is absurd. There seems an unalterable contradiction between the human mind and its employments. How can a *soul* be a merchant? What relation to an immortal being have the price of linseed, the fall of butter, the tare on tallow, or the brokerage on hemp? Can an undying creature debit 'petty expenses', and charge for 'carriage paid'? All the world's a stage; – 'the satchel, and the shining morning face' – the 'strange oaths'; – 'the bubble reputation' – the
>
> Eyes severe and beard of formal cut
> Full of wise saws and modern instances.
>
> Can these things be real? Surely they are acting. What relation have they to the truth as we see it in theory? What connection with our certain hopes? . . . The soul ties its shoe; the mind washes its hands in a basin. All is incongruous.

22 POODLE

Terry Gilliam sat in a Soho coffee bar, blue jean legs up on the seat and wondered gloomily why the world keeps asking him about the symbolism of *Jabberwocky*.

Out of the window he spotted two upright Englishmen in pin stripe suits and bowlers, noses tilted heavenward as they pushed through the crowds ignoring all around. 'That's what my films are about. They're about the eccentricities, the blind absurdity of the human race. Those men might be living on another planet.

'I don't think it's necessary to have a meaning in a film', he said. 'I think it's important to make people laugh and I seem to have done that. But there have been complaints about the gore and defecation – I had a girl from the radio interviewing me the other day demanding why I had done a film about defecation.

'It's really not quite like that but there are situations when people are very funny relieving themselves. There's nothing in the film you won't find in a Brueghel painting . . . .

There's a scene he must get into an animation some time. Walking down a street in Copenhagen he saw a very well-dressed conventional couple parading arm in arm, with them was a snowy white poodle with a plaster stuck over its bottom. 'Amazing isn't it – when I draw that people will say, "ah that's not life" '. And he chortles all the way back to Hampstead.

'Tinkling Symbols', *Guardian*, 6 April 1977.

23 HEGEL: THE GROTESQUE AS PRE- AND POST-CLASSICAL

For Bagehot, the grotesque arises out of the conflict between a Christian view of the soul and everyday commercial life. For Hegel (once again as presented by Clayborough), Christianity itself involves a view of truth which can no longer be embodied in the classical, anthropomorphic vision of Greek culture. As in pre-classical ('primitive') culture, though for very different reasons, Christian-Romantic culture breaks with the human body as model for all wholeness and unity. The grotesque, as seen from the classical perspective (which continues to govern our relationship to art at least in part, for historic – but also, we might suggest, for psychoanalytic – reasons), is the result of this break.

The section of *Time Bandits* set in Ancient Greece, where Kevin finds a bronzed, heroic father-figure in Sean Connery, is striking for its positive, un-sent-up picture of classical civilisation, and for the sadness surrounding Kevin's removal from this world by the grotesque bandit dwarfs.

Hegel distinguishes three chief kinds of art, the symbolic, the classical, and the romantic. Hegel considers this to be both the correct historical order and the ascending order of aesthetic value. He associates grotesqueness with both the symbolic and the romantic kinds of art, for reasons which a short account of his description of each kind will make clear; but it is primarily associated with symbolic art.

Each of the three kinds arises from an attempt to express the spiritual in concrete terms.

(i) Symbolic art, which is closely associated with the primitive attribution of spiritual (divine) characteristics to natural objects, attempts to represent the spiritual in distorted shapes, to express, as it were, the *super*natural by the *un*natural. Architecture, which attempts to provide a sensuous vessel for the spiritual – in the temple or church – is the fundamental type of symbolic art.

(ii) Only one shape is really 'appropriate to concrete mind', namely the human form, and 'physiology ought to have made it one of its axioms that life had necessarily in its evolution to attain to the human shape, as the sole sensuous phenomenon that is appropriate to mind'. In sculpture, the fundamental type of classical art, mind finds a satisfactory vehicle; there is a harmony of form and content. Perfect as this agreement is, however, classical art only expresses a special form of the spiritual:

> This condition has the effect that Mind is by it at once specified as a particular case of mind, the human mind, and not as simply absolute and eternal, inasmuch as mind in this latter sense is incapable of proclaiming itself otherwise than as intellectual being.

In other words, classical art can express the human mind, but not Mind, the universal and divine spirit. This is entirely suitable for the depiction of Greek gods, which are anthropomorphic: 'The Greek god is the object of naive intuition and sensuous imagination. His shape is, therefore, the bodily shape of man.'

Christianity, however, 'brings God before our intelligence as *spirit*, or mind, not as particularised individual spirit, but as absolute, in *spirit* and in truth'.

(iii) Classical art, in fact, goes as far as mere art can go. Romantic art, in attempting to represent universal Mind, in concrete terms, attempts to transcend the limitations of art. It endeavours to do this by extreme subjectivity, by reducing the external element, the medium of expression, to an absolute minimum. . . .

Grotesqueness may be associated with both the symbolic and the romantic kinds of art, for somewhat different reasons in each case. In romantic art, grotesque forms have a negative significance. They are evidence of the indifference of the spirit, as it were, to the merely phenomenal world:

> The aspect of external existence is committed to con-

tingency, and left at the mercy of freaks of the imagination, whose caprice is no more likely to mirror what is given *as* it is given, than to throw the shapes of the outer world into chance medley, or distort them into grotesqueness.

The grotesque in romantic art, then, if I understand Hegel's view correctly, reveals the presence of the spiritual much as, say, the splashing of walls and the overturning of chairs might reveal the presence of a poltergeist. Romantic art does not so much attempt an incarnation of the spiritual as a demonstration of its existence. The artist frankly despairs of finding any satisfactory concrete equivalent for the spiritual, and it is this which distinguishes the romantic from the symbolic artist.

The Time Bandits with Robin Hood (John Cleese). Handmade Films.

In symbolic art, the grotesque plays a more positive role. It is also produced by a profound dissatisfaction with natural forms; but the artist still naively hopes to find a satisfactory concrete form for the spiritual in an artistic – as distinct from a natural – shape.

The initial stage in symbolic representation is the simple charging of 'the meanest objects' with 'absolute import', for example 'when a lion is used to mean strength'. A natural object is taken as a symbol of the divine. But this being obviously unsatisfactory, because of the essential 'foreignness of the Idea to natural phenomena', the spiritual (or the Idea) – working through the artist, of course – has recourse to distortion:

> Having no other reality to express it, [it] expatiates in all these shapes, seeks itself in them in all their unrest and proportion, but nevertheless does not find them adequate to itself. Then it proceeds to exaggerate the natural shapes and the phenomena of reality into indefiniteness and disproportion, to intoxicate itself in them, to seethe and ferment in them, to do violence to them, to distort and explode them into unnatural shapes, and strives by the variety, hugeness and splendour of the forms employed to exalt the phenomenon to the level of the idea.

Clayborough, op. cit.

Hegel's idea on the grotesque might turn out to be especially useful to anyone attempting to give an account of the *positive* significance of, particularly, *Life of Brian*. For that film's power seems to go beyond its playful or satiric purposes. Despite the dislike it has aroused among religionists, it is far from clear that it is truly a post-Christian work.

24 TERRY GILLIAM NO PRAXITILES?

Time Bandits may have paid tribute to the classical ideal, but its own structural anti-classicism did not escape criticism from some reviewers, always on the look-out for 'harmony of form and content'.

Terry Gilliam's directorial debut, the extravagant *Jabberwocky*, with Michael Palin moving through the dirty old middle ages as a sort of gosh-smiley Candide, had many retching in the aisles. This column, boasting a strong stomach, found it mildly over the top excrementally but otherwise meatily funny and tremendously good-looking. *Time Bandits* is another story, if not several.

John Coleman, *New Statesman*, 17 July 1981.

The trouble with *Time Bandits* . . . is that it's too much like all the Monty Pythonery that's gone before it. . . . What the film lacks is the cohesive style to make it more than a series of extended revue sketches. . . . Mr Gilliam has the animator's flair for lightning gags and even quicker punchlines, but the episodes here are so self-contained, and their running order so academic, that there is no reason why there should not be more of them, or (as the film tends to drag at nearly two hours) fewer.

David Castell, *Sunday Telegraph*, 19 July 1981.

25 DWARFS AND THE CHILD'S-EYE VIEW

Gilliam, interviewed by Michael Watts (*The Times*, 16 July 1981), was as usual unrepentant about his cartoonist-collageist methods.

'I'd really wanted to amaze, astound and transport; in fact, to make it look like my animations. That's why I wanted "the gang" (of dwarfs); they're almost cartoon proportions. You put them against Cleese and that's an interesting picture immediately.'

A different reason for the casting of the dwarfs is added in his interview with Anne Thompson.

I wanted to do a kid's film, and all these things came out. They've obviously been storing themselves up in my head for a long time, just looking for the right outlet. I wanted to work at a kid's level through the whole thing, and the kid would be the main character. But a kid isn't going to sustain a film, so he's surrounded with a gang of interesting characters, but they've got to be the same height as the kid, so we're talking about dwarfs, folks. Step by step, it goes.

Film Comment, November/December 1981.

Interestingly, the experience of the child's-eye view also comes up in an interview with the six Time Bandits carried out by Jean Rook in the *Daily Express*, which also suggests some of the perils involved in embodying the cartoonist's ideas.

The Time Bandits are a great, international, Mini-Bond-type team. 'That worries us a bit because all dwarfs are nervous of becoming a "gang" ', admitted Dave Rappaport.

'A troop smacks of freaks and sideshows, after years of fighting to be recognised as individuals, and not just funny little men. We don't want to be labelled as The Group, however famous, though it's tempting to work together again because the film went so well.'

'It did for some', snapped Mr Ross, who broke an arm. ('You try falling off a bloody great horse that looks as high as these houses would to you!')

'The snag was the film company promised us stand-ins for the dangerous stuff', said non-swimmer Mr Purvis, who nearly drowned when he plunged into his part and a river. 'When it came to it, of course, they couldn't find stand-ins our size, so we had to do all the stunts – if you'll pardon the pun – ourselves.'

. . . One-time schoolteacher Rappaport says that seeing eye to eye, with a child, at 30, is God's greatest gift. And worth the cost of wearing doll-size hand-made suits.

'Think how marvellous it is for a grown man to be able to stand and look straight into an eight-year-old's eyes.'

Daily Express, 6 August 1981.

26 MORGENSTERN: TO SMASH LANGUAGE

Naturally the Pythons have periodically claimed not to mean anything by what they're doing (from ' "We're not satirical at all", they say. "The only intention of the show is to be funny, to make people laugh" ' – Barry Norman, *Daily Mail*, 27 December 1969 – to the endless disclaimers of any parallel between Brian and Jesus); but even when the ambition to create nonsense rather than satire has been realised, it's possible for a friendly critic to argue that the nonsense is powerfully good for society. Philip Thomson's reference in *The Grotesque* to the German nonsense poet Morgenstern is a good straightforward example of how the argument can go.

It is likely that the play-urge, the desire to invent and experiment for its own sake, is a factor in all artistic creation, but we can expect this factor to be more than usually strong in grotesque art and literature, where the breaking down and restructuring of familiar reality plays such a large part. . . . Examples of the *purely* playful grotesque are difficult to find, not surprisingly since we need some sort of drastic aspect in order to feel the presence of the truly grotesque. But even authors who indulge in seemingly harmless imaginative fun can sometimes intrude into their work rather drastic elements. . . . The Germans, who have always retained in their notion of the grotesque the element of capriciousness which Vitruvius railed against in the 'original' grotesques, class their most famous nonsense poet, Christian Morgenstern, as a grotesque writer. But Morgenstern's playfulness – like Carroll and Lear, he is fascinated by language and its vagaries – has a serious side to it. He is on record as claiming that man's basically unsatisfactory relationship to his fellows, his society and world in general stems from his being imprisoned by language, which is a most unreliable, false and dangerous thing, and that one must 'smash language', destroy man's naive trust in this most familiar and unquestioned part of his life, before he can learn to think properly. Morgenstern's brilliantly witty games with words are thus, seen from this point of view, devious devices of alienation, and at their most radical succeed in producing in the reader a strange sensation – making one suddenly doubt one's comfortable relationship with the language – not unlike the sense of disorientation and confusion associated with the grotesque.

Thomson, *The Grotesque*.

27 MONTY PYTHON BRECHTIAN?

Kristin Thompson ('Sawing Through the Bough: *Tout va bien* as a Brechtian Film', *Wide Angle* 1:3, 1976) wants to deny that *simply* 'smashing language' is a particularly progressive manoeuvre. She claims that Godard achieves an effective 'separation of filmic elements' which forces a salutary 'rethinking' on the spectator. But:

In writing this essay, I have not failed to notice that similar patterns of separation occur in a number of other works. The Monty Python movies and television series, for example, take the separation of coded elements to an even more extreme degree, mixing interviews, broadcasts, and parodies of all sorts of genres from popular narrative media. (Indeed, the television series shows a marked influence from Godard: one program cited him by including a parody of *One Plus One*).

Would we want to say that Monty Python is Brechtian? Undoubtedly not, and the reason can be found in a passage in Ben Brewster's article 'From Shklovsky to Brecht; A Reply' in the earlier Brecht issue of *Screen* (vol. 15, no. 2). There Brewster discusses Brecht's difference from the avant-garde movements of the teens and twenties:

> Brecht talked of a 'return from alienation' to distinguish his own position from that of the historical avant-gardes: 'Dadaism and surrealism use alienation-effects of the most extreme kind. Their objects do not return from alienation'. Their use of the A-effect was primitive 'because the function of this art is paralysed from the social point of view, so that here art too no longer functions. As far as its effect is concerned, it ends in an amusement.'

Thus amusement and a failure to return from alienation may mark a non-Brechtian separation of elements. Monty Python and other works may expose and parody social codes but stop at the level of amusement. Whereas *Tout va bien*, whatever humorous devices it may contain, is not ultimately comic or simply a satire of existing conventions of Hollywood romances.

The return from alienation marks a rejection of a simply absurdist view. To see the world as absurd is also to see it as incapable of change, as hopeless. The film-maker accepts political responsibility by returning from alienation. Godard and Gorin's separation of elements criticizes, but is not an absurdist condemnation.

28 REFUSING THE UPLIFTING NOTE

Where does this sort of argument leave us? Looking, possibly, for a more positive account of progressive nonsense. This is the project of Susan Stewart's *Nonsense: Aspects of Intertextuality in Folklore and Literature* (Baltimore, 1979). Stewart sees nonsense as a permanent process of putting-in-question the hierarchies, rigidities and illusions from which no human society is exempt.

The contrasts between common sense and nonsense are not so much contrasts of content as of procedure. Common sense proceeds by maximizing pattern. All social meaning is created by means of redundancy, and the verification of patterns of meaning is also the verification of patterns of social relationships . . . . This is how any truism, like the proverb, works. The utterance of 'A stitch in time saves nine' or 'You know what I mean' is a *metonymic gesture,* confirming an assumed-to-be-shared social meaning. Whether such meaning is actually shared or not is not the point; the point is the assumption and the way the assumption allows one to continue through the various dimensions of experience with privileges of signification.

Nonsense both depends upon and interrupts this metonymy . . . . Thus, although nonsense may be insulated through framing, through its status as an impossible context, its contexts are at the same time fields for the manipulation and recreation of social relationships. We have only to think of the anomaly of carnival or rites of inversion, or the calculated chaos of the 'reign of terror'. Nonsense challenges any idea of tradition as stable, as having integrity and coherence through time. This idea of tradition is manufactured by common sense with a vested interest in its own part in such a tradition. In tradition are emergent processes that are themselves counter-traditional and ambivalent, and nonsense's emergence from common sense in a replication of this process. In nonsense, hierarchies of relevance are flattened, inverted, and manipulated in a gesture that questions the idea of hierarchy itself – a gesture that celebrates an arbitrary and impermanent hierarchy. Hence the danger of nonsense not only as a valueless activity, but as an activity 'without values'. The evidence for this valueless state ranges from Colonel Streamer's 'Ruthless Rhymes for Heartless Homes' to Trotsky's worrying about the 'Bohemian nihilism' of futurism.

In nonsense, purpose becomes a continual and pleasurable movement away from itself, a reflexive gesture that spirals away from any point of privileged signification or direction. Both 'author' and 'audience' are continually fractured and rearranged. While all language assumes a possible society, while all language is *utopian*, all nonsense divides and rearranges any idea of society as coherent and integral. Nonsense threatens the disintegration of an infinite 'making conscious', an infinite movement of undercutting the world all at once and over and over again. It refuses the uplifting note by which the world assumes a happy ending.

Stewart, *Nonsense.*

By invoking 'metonymy', the figure of speech whereby the mind moves from something to something else contiguous to it, Stewart refers us to linguist Roman Jakobson's discussion of artistic realism – the construction of a 'believable' world of one-thing-next-to-another-just-where-you'd-expect-it – as a fundamentally metonymic genre. Common sense works by metonymy in that it always 'knows' what's appropriate *right here* and *next.*

What 'an infinite "making conscious" ' means is explained in the next section.

29 HYPER-CONSCIOUSNESS

This extract from Stewart should be read with those Python sketches in mind which feature characters with extraordinary abilities (like The Man Who Speaks In Anagrams) or, more commonly, extraordinary disabilities or incompetences (like the mountaineer with double vision, or the member of the Spanish Inquisition who can't say the bit about 'Our chief weapons are . . .').

The 'unconscious' as Bateson and Stewart use the term is not the Freudian unconscious; it's simply all that is not before our minds as we do things.

'Metafiction' is the type of modernist fiction intent on drawing attention to its own procedures – from Beckett and the French New Novel down to John Fowles. Stewart sees nonsense as lying beyond metafiction.

As [Gregory] Bateson has pointed out, there must be a carefully controlled economy between the conscious and the unconscious: 'It follows that all organisms must be content with rather little consciousness, and that if consciousness has any useful function whatever (which has never been demonstrated but is probably true), then *economy* in consciousness will be of first importance. No organism can afford to be conscious of matters with which it could deal at unconscious levels.'

While the interpretive activities of everyday, commonsense discourse may be seen to be selective and thus involve an implication of 'that which is not said', that which is left unrealised, such selection occurs within the realm of consciousness. What is left unsaid is assumed by members to be apparent, 'what everybody knows'. In fact, this is precisely why it is safe to allow the unsaid to remain unsaid. 'What everybody knows' is arranged hierarchically according to the contingencies of the situation at hand. To make apparent what is unnecessary to the situation, what does not need to be articulated, would be to invert this hierarchy and disintegrate the boundaries of the situation – to disintegrate the very basis of 'shared understanding' upon which the situation is constructed. Disaster would result since attention would be dispersed away from any purpose at hand, and the consequent failure to 'go on' would undermine all confidence in the viability of the given social construction of reality. This confidence would be further demoralised by a realization that once consciousness is completely made apparent, fulfilled, the unconscious is spent, made manifest, and no longer a resource. Hence the social necessity of having this remain impossible.

The potential for such a disintegration is thereby restrained to domains of the impossible context. Aesthetic activities like play and fictions take place on the interface between the conscious and unconscious. Art makes manifest aspects of the unconscious by means of skill. 'The message of skill of any sort must always be of this kind. The sensations and qualities of skill can never be put into words, and yet the fact of skill is conscious', writes Bateson. But at the same time that skill manifests aspects of the unconscious, it points to the vast potential of the unconscious – its unlimitedness. Because of this pointing towards the unconscious with a conscious gesture, and because of the ambiguous status of art as fiction – its being in and not in the world, its position on the interface of the unconscious and the conscious – the unconscious is never depleted, is never made manifest.

While texts that flaunt their fictive status make such a gesture towards this interface between consciousness and the unconscious, realism becomes more real than real to us by making some aspect of what was left unsaid in the everyday-life situation 'said'. This 'said' is accomplished by means of a metonymy that makes this revealed aspect part of a larger group of shared, though mostly unarticulated, assumptions. It is a 'said' that points to a vast and rich domain of the 'unsaid'. It is through this gesture that realism becomes 'truer' than the depicted situation. . . . The unconscious has been made conscious, but in a movement that heightens and deepens the potential of such unsaid assumptions. In this way, realism always slips into ideology – the gesture of revelation in realism is like a trigger that sets off a metonymic sequence of assumed-to-be-shared values. Realism endows social reality with a fertility and potential that would otherwise be ascribed to the unconscious. It thus gives social life over to nature, placing it in a realm beyond the control of merely human purpose and action.

But as levels of textuality move farther away from realism and towards irony and metafiction, what is 'unsaid' becomes more and more articulated, more and more a conscious matter . . . . [The text] makes conscious aspects of context that would remain unarticulated in everyday life and the fictions of realism. The text thus comes to pack its own context, to carry its own set of interpretive procedures 'spelled out' on its surface. This is the movement of nonsense with its impossible context – a context that is unrealizable, that 'no one can stand' in everyday life precisely because it is overburdened with consciousness.

. . . While we can see realism as making conscious aspects of the unconscious, it also involves the making conscious of what is potentially (although not actually) available to everyday life. There is no movement towards making conscious aspects of the text that would otherwise be left unarticulated. But texts that are *metacommunicative* involve the making conscious of skill. With increasing reflexivity, they involve a making conscious of the very procedures by which the unconscious is made conscious. With nonsense, skill itself becomes gratuitous and suspect, and is systematically inverted in a movement towards a flaunted, a *skillful*, incompetence – an incompetence that implies competence and the limits of competence with its every gesture.

Stewart, op. cit.

30 CARROT

Graham Chapman, in his first *Gay News* interview (see above, section 14), recounts a nonsense appearance at the Cambridge Union.

Not long ago I went back to Cambridge to speak at the Union, specifically because it's a place I abhor, where their up-and-coming politicians go to speak. I've always hated the place. So I went dressed as a carrot, in complete carrot costume, with a rather large yellow thing hanging down between my legs, yellow tights – the only thing you could see was the front of my face. And when it was my turn to make a speech, I said nothing. Just stood there. Stood there and said nothing. And that was my comment on the whole bloody business of people standing up and debating, trying to be clever, and eventually becoming politicians – fucking mess, they're a load of bloody idiots, and none of them have any social conscience.

I had to go on standing there beyond the point where it became embarrassing, in order for it to get embarrassing again. So I carried on standing there for a whole ten minutes, saying nothing. They laughed initially, because of the costume. They were all expecting some enormously witty remark to come out, apparently, to explain all this. But it didn't . . . . I lay down and rolled across the floor to Ivor Cutler . . . and hissed 'Get me out of this, Ivor'. So he stood up and read a poem, which nobody understood (I didn't). They were all totally bemused by what was going on. Then at least, I was able to go and sit down, in my carrot costume.

Gay News, no. 4, 1972.

31 THE INFINITY OF THE MISTAKE

Returning to Stewart:

The infinity of the mistake, of the perpetual blunder, the false step that is self-perpetuating, becomes an aspect of nonsense causality. This jump rope rhyme provides an example of this technique:

I went upstairs to make my bed;
I made a mistake and bumped my head.
I went downstairs to milk my cow;
I made a mistake and milked the sow.
I went in the kitchen to bake a pie;
I made a mistake and baked a fly.

The mistakes of the first rhyme are infinitely add-able . . . . The principle of selection is not one of common-sense actions following one another. Nor is it the 'proper not' of each action that fills the slot of 'the mistake'. Rather, out of the vast domain of 'nots' that stand opposite to the proper common-sense procedure, the jump rope performer will select an action according to a principle of rhyme. And rhyme, like phonology or punning, does not easily offer closure in terms of a common-sense idea of causality.

All . . . forms of play with infinity – nesting, circularity, the series, and the causal chain – are ways of showing the infinite connectability of all things and the arbitrariness of most connections – the mechanics of the composability that is textuality. . . . In nonsense, closure can only be imposed upon infinity by an arbitrary stop rule, a rule that says 'Enough' in a metafictive voice. If these nonsense activities show the absence and arbitrariness of all beginnings and endings, they always show the absence and arbitrariness of all middles as well. With this method of making nonsense, the center – the place of privileged signification – drops out and all that is left is a voice infinitely tracing itself into an infinite domain.

Stewart, op. cit.

The construction 'problems' that critics sometimes perceive in the Python projects and the Gilliam films can be related to this passage. The undermining of the integrity of the individual comic sketch – that is, writing sketches without always ending them 'properly' – is often instanced as *the* formal innovation in television comedy made by the Python team. This can be thought of as a move in the direction of a Larger Unity, as William Davis reports.

They defend the freeness of construction, which has become a *Python* hallmark, with the argument that it allows much more variety. 'We had the idea of a flow, one thing leading to another by association of ideas', says Terry Jones. 'The show itself has got a shape, an entity, and the components shouldn't because they break it up.'
Daily Telegraph, 21 June 1974.

On the other hand, 'sketchiness' has remained an accusation from *And Now For Something Completely Different* (Arthur Thirkell, *Daily Mirror*, 1 October 1971) –

Anarchic, eccentric British humour performed with undergrad enthusiasm is all very well in small doses, but eighty-eight minutes of unconnected lightning – and not-so-lightning – sketches begins to pall.

– to *Time Bandits* (Alexander Walker, *New Standard*, 16 July 1981 – and cf. section 24 above):

It is a rowdy pop-up chronicle with too many scenes and not all of them markedly different from each other, except in historical period. The energy of the cartoonist's drawing board keeps it going – but you grow aware there's no reason why it should ever stop.

32 PLAY, PARODY, LIST

Stewart's approach is a formalist one, in that her book is a detailed description of the formal devices by which nonsense is produced. (Nonsense doesn't just happen: you have to construct it.) Here are some more extracts. The first suggests that exaggeration, 'over-the-topness', is a message like any other. The second is concerned with the question of parody, suggesting as a test of nonsense that it cannot itself be parodied – a test which Python probably passes. The third draws an intriguing connection between Bergson's theory of comedy and the device of the comic list, so favoured by the Pythons.

I have suggested that the texts of nonsense are produced by appropriating the vertical and horizontal (or any other) organization of categories through procedures such as reversing or inverting them, shifting their boundaries, repeating them to infinity and/or exhaustion, conjoining them in time, or fracturing them into their members and recombining them according to some 'contra-sensible' principle .... The five operations I have considered are contingent upon a message 'This is play', a message that recognizes the contextual parameters of the playground. Through repeated use, such operations themselves, or a combination of them, can become contextual markers for play. Repetition, for example, seems to be a marker for play performance whenever its threat of infinity is recognized. As in the case of counting out rhymes and lullaby choruses, an exaggeration of a nonsense feature may be typical of gestures effecting absolute breaks from 'reality' to the domain of play.

Another way to transform a text by rearrangement within its boundaries is to 'pervert' it, to twist its elements into a different conclusion from the one it conventionally effects. Proverbs, those last bastions of common sense, are often the victims of this technique. This perversion can be done by rearranging the elements of the sentence: 'Better never than late', 'Time wounds all heels'. Or by eliminating elements of the proverb: 'All work and no play makes Jack'. Or by metaphoric substitutions: 'Cast thy bread upon the waters and it will come back mouldy', 'An apple a day keeps the fingers sticky'. Or by the rearrangement of two or more proverbs within one closed field: 'A stitch in time is worth two in the side', 'A stitch in time gathers no moss'. All of these perversions depend upon a knowledge of the text being manipulated and an inversion of the metaphorical power of the proverb to the literal power of nonsense . . . .

These 'perversions' can be seen as forms of parody, for parody is a matter of substituting elements within a dimension of a given text in such a way that the resulting text stands in an inverse or incongruous relation to the borrowed text . . . . Parody can only survive so long as there is common sense, so long as there is discourse that takes itself seriously. From this comes the contention that nonsense, as the outer space of the intertextual universe, cannot be parodied. Chesterton moaned in his study of Carroll that once *Alice in Wonderland* became a classic, it was no longer funny. That people had tried to parody *Alice* was symptomatic of this, and analogous to 'the comic comic strip'. And Stephen Heath has suggested that it is impossible to parody *Finnegans Wake* . . . .

Discontinuity is a way of bringing about simultaneity. The discontinuity of repetition and reversibility moves along a set of axes that begins to define a space as well as a time. Discontinuity of classification brings about an interruption and a splitting of hierarchical arrangement. Bergson noted that the reciprocal interference of series is essential to much of what is seen as comic: 'A situation is invariably comic when it belongs simultaneously to two altogether independent series of events and is capable of being interpreted in two entirely different meanings at the same time'. He concluded that the reciprocal interference of series, inversion, and repetition all consist in 'looking upon life as a repeating mechanism with reversible action and interchangeable parts'. . . . G. B. Milner, following Bergson, suggested that all 'humour-based laughter is generated by discrete elements taken, not in isolation, but in conjunction'. Within the gestalt of the discourse event, two or more domains take turns appearing and disappearing in the range of vision, and as these domains come to be farther and farther away from each other, the gestalt becomes more nonsensical. This is the nonsensical simultaneity of the list that can be a list of anything, that presents a simultaneity that is dissolvable into its disparate components. The only occasion for the meeting of the elements is a form – the list itself. This is also the nonsensical simultaneity of the pun, which places two or more distinct and disparate meanings within one simultaneous frame. While metaphor may become univocal, dissolving categories into a new category equaling more than the sum of its parts, the simultaneity of the pun is the sum of its constituent parts. The pun carries the comedy of dirt swept under a rug, which, discovered, still consists of dirt under a rug.

Stewart, op. cit.

33 IS THIS PLAY?

Two anecdotes illustrate the difficulties that can arise when the message 'This is play' isn't received. The first is told (to Sheridan Morley, in the *The Times*) by Terry Jones about his and Michael Palin's pre-Python days.

Then I got a job writing jokes for *Late Night Line Up*, of which there weren't many, so it wasn't very arduous. One night Michael and I did a sketch for the programme dressed up in Batman suits and jumping off chairs. We recorded our bit and then went home and sat by the set, surrounded by admiring or just amazed relatives. Anyway, our sketch came on and then after it they started one of those *Line Up* discussions about The Future Of The Arts or something and Dennis Potter said he hadn't come all the way from Gloucestershire to take part in a programme which could include such idiots as us. Quite soon after that I left *Line Up*.

The Times, 29 March 1975.

The second (Romany Bain, in the *Sun*) revolves around the Royal Family, presented as both not willing and very much willing to be amused (The Palace as institution vs. the Royals themselves as individuals).

Anything can happen when the Monty Python gang are around.

At the premiere of their film *Monty Python and The Holy Grail* . . . they planned to present their eight-foot-tall 'dummy Princess Margaret', who appeared in so many sketches.

But EMI Film Distributors got cold feet about the idea and called the Palace.

'They were told by a spokesman that the Palace was not very keen', says 34-year-old Pythoneer Graham Chapman.

Terry Jones, 31, also in the Python team, says: 'I'm sure it wasn't the Princess who objected. At our Drury Lane show last year, the dummy HRH was sitting in the Royal Box and the real Princess seemed to enjoy it.'

Sun, 29 March 1975.

34 PRANKS AND CRIMES

One final extract from Stewart, still on the subject of the 'frame' that allows nonsense to transgress social codes without it quite counting (although the grotesque effect arises to the degree that, as in the Chapman story in section 30 above, it *almost threatens to count*).

Reversibility may be a characteristic of our perception of culture in general, and particularly of the idea of culture as communication. While we see the natural world as constant – unchanged by the desires and purposes of human activities except in so far as human activities interrupt or interfere with the natural order – we see culture as constantly in process, transformable, and manipulable when considered as a process of communication. This point is implied by Lévi-Strauss's statement that one could limit 'the expression "structures of subordination" by opposing it to "structures of communication"; meaning thereby that there are, in society, two major structural types; structures of communication which are reciprocal and structures of subordination, on the other hand, which are univocal and not reversible.' This distinction between reversible and nonreversible structures not only holds against the intertextual division between realism (univocal and nonreversible) and irony/metafiction (multivocal and reversible), it is also symptomatic of a more basic division between fictive and nonfictive events in social life. Nonfictive events are those that happen in social time, that 'really did occur' and cannot be 'taken back'. In contrast, fictive events are framed as reversible events. They can be taken back by saying 'This is just a story', or 'I was just joking', by asserting their paradoxical is/is not status as events and nonevents. This basic division is evident in games where there is a period that 'does not count' and where scores can be reversed back to zero. Here the text of experience virtually can be erased. When experience 'really counts', nothing can be done to reverse its ongoingness. The whole domain of 'practice', however, gives us another example of a fictive domain, a domain that can be reversed. And from the previous discussion of nonsense and learning, we can see that the reverse – that all fictions are practice domains – may be true as well.

This fundamental distinction between nonfictive and fictive events is further demonstrated in the way we classify pranks and crimes. The interface between pranks and crimes is determined by the reversibility of their effects. Soap can be washed off windows, paint can be sand-blasted, windows can be replaced, but scars and death are not held to be reversible. 'Hurt' is defined in terms of the body's capabilities to reverse damage. When fraternity members get their heads shaved during 'rush', they have confidence that their hair will grow back. It is interesting that when fraternity pranks do result in serious injury or death, it is not the activity 'pranks' that is blamed, but the failure in classification. To say 'They do not know when to stop' is to say that the fraternity members passed 'a point of no return', a point where reversible actions become irreversible because of an error in framing. When people make continued classificatory errors of this type they move from being a prankster to a delinquent, and their participation in social life is forcibly restricted.

Stewart, op. cit.

Monty Python's Life of Brian. Handmade Films.

Outside the frame, meanwhile, matters can get out of hand in Milford Haven:

Groups of Mods and Rockers who went on the rampage at Milford Haven on Saturday evening may have been angry at a ban on the film *Life of Brian* from local cinemas.

This is one theory being considered by police at the oil port who spent yesterday investigating a serious crime wave which included an attack on a 14-year-old boy, vehicles being stolen, windows smashed, burglaries, and a spate of sign daubing on shops and public buildings . . . .

Presell District Council's decision to ban the Monty Python film could have been partially responsible, as several of the signs sprayed with paint on buildings declared, 'Brian lives on'.

Milford Haven's Town Hall, a local supermarket, a church meeting place and Hakin bridge were among the places selected for graffiti and the daubers also painted obscenities about the council . . . .

Western Mail, 21 April 1980.

35 ALMOST A NORMAL PERSON

Creating nonsense and operating over the edge of the grotesque must induce a desire to work sometimes in a quite different area. But of course the Pythons do, as entrepreneurs of their own talents, and, increasingly, as a force in the British cinema. Chris Greenwood describes the business in which John Cleese has chosen to near-normalise himself.

At one end of the phone is John Cleese, hair slicked down Adolf Hitler-style, voice pitched at an officious and unhelpful whine, pencil crawling at snail's pace across the page.

He's the obstructive clerk who sticks to the rule book even if it does mean losing a sale.

Bawling at him is the customer, Ronnie Barker, purple with frustration as he tries to order a new part for a machine.

It's British comedy at its best, yet ironically this scene will never flicker across the screens at our Odeons or Rialtos. Nor will it make television.

For this little epic, starring Cleese and Barker, is a training film. The audiences for such films consists of exclusive groups of company executives, accountants, secretaries and sales staff, the idea being to show them how to improve relationships between themselves and their customers, how to understand finance and balance sheets, and take decisions – in that film Cleese appears as Queen Elizabeth I to illustrate the point . . . .

The films are didactic by nature and intent, but the message isn't bashed home. It slides in between the ribs as they're being tickled.

Some training films are sponsored by big companies like Shell and are shown for public relations motives. At the other end of the spectrum are companies like Video Arts, Rank Aldis and Cygnet Guild who are in it purely for the money. Their turnover is an estimated £6 million annually.

Video Arts is masterminded by Antony Jay, former editor of *Tonight* and onetime head of BBC's Talks Features department . . . .

Jay had met Cleese while writing for the *Frost Report*. They set to work on a training film script, which was shot in the summer of '72, directed by Peter Robinson, and is still a firm seller today. . . .

If Cleese had not been financially involved in Video Arts, it's unlikely we would ever have enjoyed the superb farce of *Fawlty Towers*. When Cleese sat down with his ex-wife Connie Booth to write the second half-dozen Fawltys his split was £1000 an episode.

'It took 36 weeks in all, a total of six weeks an episode for a thousand quid a time', he said. 'If it hadn't been for my Video Arts income and the odd Sony commercial I'd have had to sell my house.'

Cleese finds the training films a refreshing break. 'Viewers who watched me in *Python* thought I was completely mad', he said. 'And those who liked *Fawlty Towers* assumed I was like Basil.

'The business people who see these films regard me as almost a normal person.' . . .

Daily Mail, 17 August 1981.

36 ARMS OFF/HANDMADE

John Walker in the *Sunday Express Magazine* provides a summary of the practical plans of Handmade Films at the same time as getting us back to the grotesque and the medieval as favoured by Terry Gilliam. (Castration meets The Industry?)

[Gilliam] wrote scripts for two unexpected films, but failed to get financial backing for them. One, set in the near future, 'has insanity as a happy ending'. The other concerns Theseus and the Minotaur, taking its inspiration from G. F. Watts' Victorian painting in the Tate Gallery of the sad monster, a small bird crushed under one hoof, looking bleakly out over a parapet. . . .

Palin and Gilliam have brought different strengths to the film. Palin's talent is for a gentle, atmospheric approach to humour. Gilliam's is much tougher, characterised by those enormous feet that would crush the life out of his animations in *Monty Python*.

There's no mistaking his jokes in *Time Bandits*: in a brief moment of arm-wrestling at Robin Hood's camp the winner wrenches off his opponent's arm. And one of the dwarfs, Vermin, is omnivorous, munching candles and even the head off a rat.

'The RSPCA or the Royal Society For The Prevention Of Arms Coming Off should complain to Terry', says Palin. 'His humour does have a savage edge. But I like it, because if we did my stuff all the time, it would be slightly soft.'

The outgoing Gilliam – 'I'm an adrenalin freak' – revels in medieval life. His favourite artists are Brueghel and Bosch. 'Imagination ran riot in the Middle Ages. The grotesque wasn't seen as abnormal. Then people did not seem ashamed of any aspect of life. You can go into magnificent churches and find carvings of people doing really gross things.'

Gilliam enjoys probing humour to its limits. An American who came to England 14 years ago in pursuit of a love affair, he feels sentimental about London. . . .

Gilliam and the other Pythons are helping to boost the British film industry. When Lord Delfont withdrew EMI's backing from *Monty Python's Life of Brian*, the necessary finance was raised by [*Time Bandits'* co-producers Denis] O'Brien and [ex-Beatle George] Harrison, who mortgaged his house.

The company they formed, Handmade Films, plans to produce three big British films a year, including the next Monty Python opus. And the Python team are shareholders with O'Brien and Harrison in a distribution company whose first success was buying the thriller *The Long Good Friday* from Lord Grade, who planned to cut the film for showing on television.

'Our hope is that Handmade can help distribute films that the big two distributors turn down', says Palin, who is also on the board of Shepperton Studios. 'I believe in things like cinemas and railways. There was a time when every town had the choice of four or five cinemas. Now it's rather like television: cinema is served up with the choice of two channels.'

Sunday Express Magazine, 12 July 1981.

37 BAKHTIN: LIBERATING GROTESQUE

Any explanation of the Pythons' immensely outgoing and productive collective and individual careers that misses out the energy they have drawn from the grotesque is clearly defective.

The great Russian critic Mikhail Bakhtin, in *Rabelais and His World* (tr. Helene Iswolsky, Cambridge, Mass., 1968) celebrates and analyses the grotesque elements in Rabelais with exemplary generosity. He stresses that the gloomy, anxious origins of the grotesque (psychological and sociological) are not perpetuated by it but are transcended by it. He takes Wolfgang Kayser, author of an influential German work on the subject, to task for projecting on to the medieval grotesque a characteristically Romantic gloom.

Another of Kayser's definitions is characteristic of the modernist interpretation: 'the grotesque is a form expressing the *id*'.

The *id* is understood by the author not so much in the Freudian as in the existentialist sense of this word. *Id* is an alien, inhuman power, governing the world, men, their life and behavior. Kayser reduces many of the basic grotesque themes to the realization of this power, for instance the puppet theme. He also reduces to this power the theme of madness. According to the author we are always aware of something alien in the madman, as if some inhuman spirit of irony had entered his soul. We have already said that the theme of madness is used in the grotesque in quite a different manner – to escape the false 'truth of this world' in order to look at the world with eyes free from this 'truth'. . . .

Actually the grotesque liberates man from all the forms of inhuman necessity that direct the prevailing concept of the world. This concept is uncrowned by the grotesque and reduced to the relative and the limited. Necessity, in every concept which prevails at any time, is always one-piece, unconditional, and indisputable. But historically the idea of necessity is relative and variable. The principle of laughter and the carnival spirit on which grotesque is based destroys this limited seriousness and all pretense of an extratemporal meaning and unconditional value of necessity. It frees human consciousness, thought, and imagination for new potentialities. For this reason great changes, even in the field of science, are always preceded by a certain carnival consciousness that prepares the way.

In the grotesque world the *id* is uncrowned and transformed into a 'funny monster'. When entering this new dimension, even if it is Romantic, we always experience a peculiar gay freedom of thought and imagination.

Bakhtin, *Rabelais and His World*.

38 THE GROTESQUE BODY

Bakhtin's description of the grotesque body (which might be compared with material in sections 10, 11, 12, and 15 above) brings out how under carnivalesque conditions the fear of one's body's boundaries becoming fluid turns into exhilaration. The grotesque is a celebratory overturning of classical form (cf. Hegel, section 23 above). It is as if the infant as described by Melanie Klein has, with full adult confidence and courage, *accepted* its early terrors, laughingly.

We find at the basis of grotesque imagery a special concept of the body as a whole and of the limits of this whole. The confines between the body and the world and between separate bodies are drawn in the grotesque genre quite differently than in the classic and naturalistic images. . . .

Of all the features of the human face, the nose and mouth play the most important part in the grotesque image of the body; the head, ears, and nose also acquire a grotesque character when they adopt the animal form or that of inanimate objects. The eyes have no part in these comic images; they express an individual, so to speak, self-sufficient human life, which is not essential to the grotesque. The grotesque is interested only in protruding eyes. . . . It is looking for that which protrudes from the body, all that seeks to go out beyond the body's confines. Special attention is given to the shoots and branches, to all that prolongs the body and links it to other bodies or to the world outside. Moreover, the bulging eyes manifest a purely bodily tension. But the most important of all human features for the grotesque is the mouth. It dominates all else. The grotesque face is actually reduced to the gaping mouth; the other features are only a frame encasing this wide-open bodily abyss.

The grotesque body . . . is a body in the act of becoming. It is never finished, never completed; it is continually built, created, and builds and creates another body. Moreover, the body swallows the world and is itself swallowed by the world. . . . This is why the essential role belongs to those parts of the grotesque body in which it outgrows its own self, transgressing its own body, in which it conceives a new, second body: the bowels and the phallus. These two areas play the leading role in the grotesque image, and it is precisely for this reason that they are predominantly subject to positive exaggeration, to hyperbolization; they can even detach themselves from the body and lead an independent life, for they hide the rest of the body, as something secondary. (The nose can also in a way detach itself from the body.) Next to the bowels and the genital organs is the mouth, through which enters the world to be swallowed up. And next is the anus. All these convexities and orifices have a common characteristic; it is within them that the confines between bodies and between the body and the world are overcome: there is an interchange and an interorientation. This is why the main events in the life of the grotesque body, the acts of the bodily drama, take place in this sphere. Eating, drinking, defecation and other elimination (sweating, blowing of the nose, sneezing), as well as copulation, pregnancy, dismemberment, swallowing up by another body – all these acts are performed on the confines of the body and the outer world, or on the confines of the old and new body. In all these events the beginning and end of life are closely linked and interwoven.

Thus the artistic logic of the grotesque image ignores the closed, smooth, and impenetrable surface of the body and retains only its excrescences (sprouts, buds) and orifices, only that which leads beyond the body's limited space or into the body's depths. Mountains and abysses, such is the relief of the grotesque body; or speaking in architectural terms, towers and subterranean passages.

Bakhtin, op. cit.

Bakhtin adds a footnote to the penultimate sentence: 'This grotesque logic is also extended to images of nature and of objects in which depths (holes) and convexities are emphasized.'

39 COSMIC TERROR, MATERIALIST RESPONSE

With an imaginative leap Bakhtin connects certain scatological themes in the medieval grotesque with the overcoming of a specific sort of fear.

We must not forget that urine (as well as dung) is gay matter, which degrades and relieves at the same time, transforming fear into laughter. If dung is a link between body and earth (the laughter that unites them), urine is a link between body and sea . . . . Dung and urine lend a bodily character to matter, to the world, to the cosmic elements, which becomes closer, more intimate, more easily grasped, for this is the matter, the elemental force, born from the body itself. It transforms cosmic terror into a gay carnival monster.

We must take into consideration the importance of cosmic terror, the fear of the immeasurable, the infinitely powerful. . . . This cosmic terror is not mystic in the strict sense of the word; rather it is the fear of that which is materially huge and cannot be overcome by force. It is used by all religious systems to oppress man and his consciousness. Even the most ancient images of folklore express the struggle against fear, against the memories of the past, and the apprehension of future calamities, but folk images relating to this struggle helped develop true human fearlessness. The struggle against cosmic terror in all its forms and manifestations did not rely on abstract hope or on the eternal spirit, but on the material principle in man himself. Man assimilated the cosmic elements: earth, water, air, and fire; he discovered them and became vividly conscious of them in his own body. . . . We must here stress that it was in the material acts and eliminations of the body – eating, drinking, defecation, sexual life – that man found and retraced within himself the earth, sea, air, fire, and all the cosmic matter and its manifestations, and was thus able to assimilate them. Indeed, the images of the material bodily lower stratum have a prevailing cosmic connotation.

Animation by Terry Gilliam for *Monty Python's Flying Circus*. BBC/Python (Monty) Pictures Ltd.

In a footnote Bakhtin elaborates on what he means by 'cosmic terror' and how it differs from infant terror of the Kleinian sort.

The images reflecting this struggle are often interwoven with images of a parallel struggle in the individual body against the memories of an agonising birth and the fear of the throes of death. Cosmic fear is deeper and more essential. It is hidden in the ancestral body of mankind; this is why it has penetrated to the very basis of language, imagery, and thought. This cosmic terror is more essential and stronger than individual bodily fear of destruction, though both voices often mingle in folklore and especially in literature. Cosmic terror is the heritage of man's ancient impotence in the presence of nature. Folk culture did not know this fear and overcame it through laughter, through lending a bodily substance to nature and the cosmos; for this folk culture was always based on the indestructible confidence in the might and final victory of man. Official culture, on the contrary, often used and even cultivated this fear in order to humiliate and oppress man.

Bakhtin, op. cit.

40 DISMEMBERMENT

Again, what Bakhtin has to say on this theme makes an interesting contrast to Lacan's doctrine (cf. section 10 above).

In medieval literature the dismembered bodies of saints were often an occasion for grotesque images and enumerations. In one of the best medieval parodies, 'The Treatise of García of Toledo' . . . the hero, a wealthy simonist bishop from Toledo, brings to Rome a present for the Pope, the miraculous relics of the saintly martyrs Ruphinus and Albinus. In the language of medieval travesties the names of these nonexistent saints mean gold and silver. The story describes the Pope's particular devotion to the martyrs. He praises them and asks that all their precious remains should be brought to him; there follows a grotesque enumeration of the various parts of the dismembered bodies: 'from Ruphinus' kidneys, Albinus' intestines, from stomach, back, rump, ribs, chest, legs, and arms; and all the members of the saints.' We see that, as early as the eleventh century, relics were the object of parody.

. . . From the thirteenth century on, a poem entitled 'The Ass's Will' was widely known in Europe. A dying ass bequeaths the parts of his body to various social and professional groups, beginning with the Pope and cardinals. The dismemberment here corresponds to the divisions of the social hierarchy: the ass's head is for the Pope, the ears for the cardinals, the voice for the choir, the feces for the peasants, etc. . . .

In these satires it is interesting to note the combination of the dismemberment of the body and of society. This is a travesty of the widespread mythical concept of the origin of various social groups from various parts of a god's body. (The oldest monument of this social topography is the *Rig-Veda*.) In most cases this is a dismembered body. But here, instead of a god's body, we have the body of an ass; this is an ancient traditional travesty of the divinity. In medieval parodies its organs and its braying, as well as the shouts of its drivers, play an important part. We hear these shouts in Rabelais' novel. There are several mentions of the abusive term: '*viédaze*', the ass's phallus. . . .

There is more on the dismembered culture hero in a Bakhtin footnote:

The *Rig-Veda* pictures the birth of the world from the body of the man Purusha; the gods sacrificed him and cut up his body, according to the method of sacrificial dismemberment. Various social groups were thus created from the various parts of Purusha's body, as well as from certain cosmic phenomena. From his mouth appeared the Brahmans, from his arms soldiers, from his eyes the sun, from his head the sky, from his feet the earth, etc. In the christianized Germanic mythology we find a similar conception, but here the body is composed of the various parts of the universe. Adam's body is composed of flesh from the earth, bones from stones, blood from the sea, hair from plants, and thoughts from clouds.

Bakhtin, op. cit.

41 A NEST OF MAGPIE CLUTTER

Perhaps this is a good point to remind ourselves of how the grotesquerie of Gilliam's imagination (and of his studio), as reported by Bevis Hillier, compares with the archaic material Bakhtin is discussing.

Gilliam is the artist who gave *Monty Python's Flying Circus* its sinister animation sequences, including the obliterating naked foot which stamped down like a steam hammer on figures and landscapes, crushing them into the ground. That nude leg, I had not realised, was neatly amputated by Gilliam from the cupid of Bronzino's *Venus and Cupid* in the National Gallery.

No. 147. *The Pope-afs.*

Illustration from *A History of Caricature and Grotesque* by Thomas Wright, London 1865.

'Taking something out of context gives me more pleasure than anything else. People are amazed. They think: "That silly foot!" ' His American parents still wonder where he got 'all those terrible ideas which came out in the cartoons' . . . ideas like a Pinocchio-hatted executioner chopping a cow in half lengthwise, to reveal a hollow shell like the inside of a rubber ball; a swarm of suburban houses flying through the air and about to alight on an unspoilt Green Belt hillside; a Freud knitting with his feet; an angel emerging from a pair of grotesque, booted haunches which squats on a fizzing time-bomb planet; an Amazonian woman detonating her breasts.

Of these sinister notions their creator says: 'Very cathartic. Cheaper than psychoanalysis, less dangerous than attacking people on street corners.' But television is a fleeting medium and its freshest ideas are soon just a memory. To those hungering for a new dose of Gilliam's fancies, he is now offering *Animations of Mortality*, a printed collection of new work along with some Monty Python pieces. . . .

The room Gilliam works in is not in fact small. It is at the top of the Victorian house in Hampstead where he lives with his wife Maggie (a make-up expert) and two-year-old daughter Amy Rainbow. It is a nest of magpie clutter: a urinal fitted with a doll's head and limbs, a terracotta gargoyle from a Victorian convent, old iron shoe lasts, a pin machine, Chinese kites and a harmonium with a sheet of ragtime on the music-stand.

Ropes of creeper strong enough for Tarzan to swing on hang from a minstrel's gallery. On the walls are reproductions of the artists Gilliam admires: Hieronymous Bosch, inevitably, Salvador Dali, Max Ernst. . . .

Sunday Telegraph Supplement, 24 October 1978.

42 CARNIVALISATION OF SPEECH

Rabelais himself seems as much a verbal precursor of Python as a whole as Brueghel and Bosch are visual precursors. Bakhtin again:

One of the popular forms of comic speech was the so-called *coq-à-l'âne*, 'from rooster to ass'. This is a genre of intentionally absurd verbal combinations, a form of completely liberated speech that ignores all norms, even those of elementary logic.

. . . The speeches of Kissarse, Bumfondle, and Pantagruel in the episode of the lawsuit offer the purest, one might say classic *coq-à-l'âne*. The speeches are not a parody of the legal eloquence of that time, nor are they, generally speaking, a parody at all. The images chosen for the speeches are devoid of all visible links. Here is the beginning of Kissarse's speech:

> My Lord, the truth is that a good woman of my house was taking her eggs to market. . . .
>
> *Whereas* there passed between the twin tropics the sum of threepence towards the zenith . . . and *whereas* the Riphaean Mountains had that year suffered a great sterility of paste and imitation stone . . . and *whereas* this was due to a warfare of fiddlefaddle seditiously fomented between the tripegabblers and the Accursian maunder-mongers . . . and *whereas* the cause of the contention was the rebellion of the Switzers, who had assembled to the number of three, six, nine, ten . . . and *whereas* they did this to get presents on New Year's day, at the season when soup is served to oxen and the keys of the coal cellar given to country wenches so they may feed the dogs plenty of oats. . . .
>
> . . . all night long they kept their hands on the pot, dispatching Bulls on horseback and Bulls on foot to keep the ships in harbour, because the tailors insisted on making stolen tatters into
>
> A peashooter to shoot a pea
> Across the Oceanic Sea
>
> which at the moment was pregnant with a potful of cabbage, according to the opinion handed down by the manufacturers of hay-bundles. On the contrary, the physicians maintained that the urine revealed no positive traces. . . .
>
> (Book 2, Chapter 11)

As we pointed out, there is no link between these images; Kissarse's speech truly skips from 'rooster to ass'. It is built in the spirit of the Russian proverb: 'In the vegetable garden grows the elder tree, and uncle is in Kiev.' But all these jumbled images are offered according to the Rabelaisian system. We have here the typical grotesque picture of the world, in which the generating, devouring, and defecating body is fused with nature and with cosmic phenomena. . . . We further see various kitchen and household materials and activities in their carnivalesque aspect (soup served to oxen, the feeding of oats to dogs). Finally, all these grotesque bodily, cosmic, and carnivalesque images are combined with historic events (the rebellion of the Switzers, the dispatching of Bulls to keep the ships in harbour). All these images and the very mode of their combination are typical of popular-festive forms. . . .

In a period of the radical breaking up of the world's hierarchical picture and the building of a new concept, leading to a revision of all old words, objects, and ideas, the *coq-à-l'âne* acquired an essential meaning; it was a form which granted momentary liberation from all logical links – a form of free recreation. It was, so to speak, the carnivalization of speech, which freed it from the gloomy seriousness of official philosophy as well as from truisms and commonplace ideas. This verbal carnival broke man's century-old chains of medieval philosophy, thus preparing a new sober seriousness.

Bakhtin, op. cit.

43 THE SERIO-LOOPY

One of the best critical evocations so far of the feel of Python Rabelaisianism in action has been Penelope Gilliatt's *New Yorker* review of *Monty Python and the Holy Grail*, which also ties in with Stewart's remarks (above, section 31) on mistakes.

If the film can be said to have a theme, it has three. These are swallows, mud, and the Grail. Swallows keep recurring. So does mud, and all manner of other dirt. The King is brusquely recognised as being quite likely to be a king because he hasn't got mud on his clothes. There is also a certain amount of wistfully lewd talk from eight-score young and cloistered medieval blondes (some with 'basic medical training') when they see one of King Arthur's knights. And a very large number of mud-soaked animal corpses are thrown from castle battlements, all with a strong look of being the works of a taxidermist so abysmally uninterested in his job that he never reached second-year apprenticeship. As to the Grail, the quest for that leads every which way, because no one seems at all certain what he is looking for. . . . The thought that the Grail is the third theme brings to mind a fine scene in which Scriptural advice about counting to three in launching a Holy Hand Grenade is taken as a text by some very etiolated-looking monks:

> And the Lord spake, saying, first shalt thou take out the Holy Pin, then shalt thou count to three, no more, no less. Three shall be the number thou shalt count, and the number of the counting shall be three. Four shalt thou not count, neither count thou two, excepting that thou then proceed to three. . . . Once the number three, being the third number, be reached, then lobbest thou thy Holy Hand Grenade of Antioch toward the foe, who, being naughty in my sight, shall croak.

This is a typical quote from the film, which belongs to a serio-loopy school of one. So are the strange oaths that John Cleese as an Anglophobic Frenchman levels at King Arthur and his band ('English k-niggets! . . . Sons of a window-dresser!'), and a scrap of chatty scientific counselling held en route to somewhere or other that marks England's emergence from the Dark Ages. (Sir Tristram: 'And that, my Lord, is how we know the earth to be banana-shaped.' King Arthur: 'This new learning amazes me, Sir Tristram. Explain again how sheeps' bladders may be employed to prevent these so-called earthquakes.'). . . . The whole film, which is often recklessly funny and sometimes a matter of comic genius, is a triumph of errancy and muddle. Its mind strays like an eye, and it thrives on following false trails. The Monty Python people have won a peculiar right to be funny even when they make a mess of things, because their style accepts floundering as a condition of life.

New Yorker, 5 May 1975.

44 THE CHORUS OF THE LAUGHING PEOPLE

Bakhtin concludes *Rabelais and His World* with a directly political defence of the Rabelaisian: it gave, for once, a lasting form to the popular scepticism, wit, resistance which so often leaves no cultural landmarks and yet is so important a stratum of history.

Our study is only a first step in the vast task of examining ancient folk humour and even as a first step possibly may not be sufficiently firm and correct. But we are profoundly convinced of the importance of this task. We cannot understand cultural and literary life and the struggle of mankind's historic past if we ignore that peculiar folk humor that always existed and was never merged with the official culture of the ruling classes.

Monty Python's Life of Brian. Handmade Films.

While analyzing past ages we are too often obliged to 'take each epoch at its word', that is, to believe its official ideologists. We do not hear the voice of the people and cannot find and decipher its pure unmixed expression.

All the acts of the drama of world history were performed before a chorus of the laughing people. Without hearing this chorus we cannot understand the drama as a whole. Let us imagine Pushkin's *Boris Godunov* without the scenes involving the massed people; such a conception of Pushkin's drama would be not only incomplete but distorted. Each character in the play expresses a limited point of view. The authentic meaning of the epoch and its events is disclosed in these crowd scenes, where Pushkin lets the people have the last word.

Our example is not merely a metaphoric comparison. In all periods of the past there was the marketplace with its laughing people, that very marketplace that in Pushkin's drama appeared in the pretender's nightmare:

> The people swarmed on the public square
> And pointed laughingly at me,
> And I was filled with shame and fear.

We repeat, every act of world history was accompanied by a laughing chorus. But not every period of history had Rabelais for coryphaeus. Though he led the popular chorus of only one time, the Renaissance, he so fully and clearly revealed the peculiar and difficult language of the laughing people that his work sheds its light on the folk culture of humor belonging to other ages.

Bakhtin, op. cit.

45 ON THE SIDE OF LIBERTY

Reviewing *And Now For Something Completely Different*, Penelope Gilliatt perceived the libertarian strand running through the Python sketches.

The world of *And Now For Something Completely Different* is all on the side of liberty, and notes with a basilisk eye any incursions of English authoritarianism. There is a good deal of material about the sort of people who are always seeing burglars and other dangerous party-groupists (foreigners, the young, and so on) under the bed. One singular sketch is about the peril to the public of mad forays by grannies on the prowl. . . .

English bureaucratic sloth is one of the continuing butts of the film. So is the propaganda style used in the Second World War, which the writers and actors . . . take to be so much garbage. There is a flash of sober official advice about how to kill enemy Germans with jokes. . . . These *new* jokes, reports the commentator in the voice of wartime British newsreels, are over ten thousand times as powerful as the prewar jokes used at Munich. Nothing is sacrosanct in *And Now For Something Completely Different* . . . least of all patriotism and any sort of bigotry.

New Yorker, 26 August 1972.

Richard Schickel in *Time* magazine notes that *Monty Python and the Holy Grail* is determinedly anti-war. (The connections between the Python ethos and World War/Cold War weariness would be worth examining; perhaps the most bizarre of these involves John Cleese's family name. This used to be Cheese, but his father changed it upon enlisting in World War I, fearing ridicule.)

Arthur's adventures reach no logical conclusion. They are simply brought to an abrupt end when a police car rolls up and the entire Round Table is rounded up. . . . The intervention of the bobbies also leads to the fine sight of a fully armored knight being spread-eagled against the squad car and being patted down for concealed weapons.

This is a key image in the film, which pats down the entire chivalric tradition for bloody and dangerous residual ideas. Along with the high comedy, this determined insistence on the gory stupidity of ancient but still potent fancy is what holds the film together. *Grail* is as funny as a movie can get, but it is also a tough-minded picture – as outraged about the human propensity for violence as it is outrageous in its attack on that propensity.

Time, 26 May 1975.

46 VIEWS FROM ABROAD

Perhaps Python humour is easier to perceive as salutarily savage from abroad. P. D. Zimmerman had already given *Time* readers a class-struggle view of Pythonism which seems not quite right but not quite wrong either.

And Now For Something Completely Different dances gleefully on the grave of upper-crust English institutions and moribund Establishment mores. . . . The stiff-upper-lip sort of British Blimp gets the worst of it, but every social class goes under attack – for, as in any wild comedy assault, the cry here is anarchy.

. . . This cavalcade of insanity climaxes with 'Upper Class Twit of the Year', an Olympics for catatonic and demented aristocrats, which locates the film as part of that ongoing under-class revolution that exploded in the late 1950s. It is a specifically British obsession, this flogging of the privileged class – but it is so wildly, spastically played that, like the entire flim, it transcends its cultural context. . . .

Time, 4 September 1972.

How and why Python jokes travel are interesting questions. The following piece by Martin Roth in the *Sunday Times*, while firmly in the funny-foreigners journalistic tradition, does make one wonder about Python in Japan.

There are problems with jokes from the mysterious west. The audience roared with laughter at the Television Blackmail Game and the Upper Class Twit of the Year Race, but seemed bewildered by the 'nudge nudge' and dead parrot sketches. 'We Japanese wouldn't argue so much if a product was unsatisfactory', a Tokyo girl told me.

The film's importer, Telecas Japan, helped the audiences to leap the humour barrier by preparing a 20-page programme . . . which relentlessly 'explains' every scene. (Sample: 'It is the middle of a Canadian forest: in natural surroundings a lumberjack cuts down big trees, but in reality he is a homosexual.')

The programme also has two highbrow essays on the nature of satire and on the success of Monty Python. (. . . 'To understand black humour we need political understanding; but Japanese people do not concern themselves with politics in their daily lives, so they do not understand the black humour or the anger of Monty Python.')

Sunday Times, 30 March 1980.

American novelist Thomas Berger, writing in *Esquire*, uses the opening sketch of *And Now For Something Completely Different* as a way into thinking about certain Anglo-American cultural differences.

The opening scene shows a wooden landscape devoid of people, but an unseen commentator assures us that forty-seven human beings are concealed there, and identifies the first of them by name and address – which, as often in British comedy, are funny in themselves, especially the address, from which any Englishman can immediately identify, as he can from an accent, the class and perhaps even the profession of the person who belongs to it. This can rarely be done in mobile, unstructured American, and is seldom attempted in the interests of comedy except in the old war movies in which GIs named 'Brooklyn' and 'Texas' invariably spoke, in the wrong accents, dialogue utterly unevocative of place, but were supposed to be hilarious by naked definition. (Lyndon Johnson, on the other hand, performing with genuine voice and references in the farce called politics, was despised for his authenticity.)

But to get back to the opening . . . given a local habitation and a name, and summoned by the commentator to show himself, the man rises from a depression in the earth and is immediately shot down. Identification evokes instant obliteration. 'This demonstrates', says the disembodied voice, 'the virtue of not being seen'.

Esquire, December 1972.

47 FILMED ENTIRELY ON WOOD

In the autumn of 1980, *Life of Brian* well behind them, the Python team found themselves performing live in America for the first time since 1976: they did four hugely successful shows at the Hollywood Bowl. Steve Pond interviewed various Pythons for *Rolling Stone* as well as covering the event.

'I don't know if the others have told you the truth', John Cleese says as he pulls me into an empty booth inside the Bowl and leans foward conspiratorially. 'The real reason we're playing the Hollywood Bowl is that we're absolutely stuck on our next movie. We spent thirteen weeks writing, but we just don't have a central theme. We've got scenes set in 1980 and 1880, in England and in British India, but nothing ties them together. So I moved that we abandon the project for a good lump of time, and when we get back to it next September, maybe we'll have come up with a plot.

'But that left us with our falls free', he continues, 'facing the prospect of having worked for three months without making a penny. It made sense to do these shows: we're able to come to Los Angeles, have a holiday in the sun and make enough money to tide us over.'

Cleese . . . adds that he wasn't opposed to simply writing a film of unconnected sketches. The others, though, felt that *Life of Brian* – unlike, say, the somewhat disjointed *Holy Grail* – had set a standard they couldn't ignore. 'The stage of making sketch films is past', says Cleese. 'You've got to keep the audience on the hop a bit, not let them get ahead of you.' . . .

Later, I get a differing opinion on the movie from Graham Chapman. . . . 'I think we do have something of a linking factor', he says. 'Sex and violence.' . . .

As they sit in the restaurant back at the hotel, Palin and Jones agree that Python's slow pace is healthy. 'We live in a strange way, Python', says Palin. . . . 'One of our virtues is that we don't sign any contracts over how much work we should do. We can't just churn the stuff out.

'That's why we delayed the film. . . . We could have had a movie out by the end of the year, if we'd been content with a certain standard. But we have to be careful not to parody our own style.'

'On the television show, we found a new form for TV comedy', adds Jones. . . . 'Now we're looking for a new form for film.'

'Like wood', Palin offers. 'Filmed entirely on *wood*. The projectionists hate it, because it makes no impression on the screen and it ruins their equipment. *Gone are the shoddy restrictions of celluloid. . . .*'

Palin picks up where he left off. 'So we can all afford to take a year off and do our own things. We certainly couldn't organise our lives around Python. We get together when we want to, not out of a sense of duty.'

'Except the *Contractual Obligation Album*', laughs Jones.

'Well, yes. We knew there was no way out of that one', says Palin. 'They sent around a man in a black mask with a gun, and he said, "Give us an album or the kids get it".' . . .

[On the album the Pythons] do sing – fifteen times, far more than on any previous outing. Chapman drew on his medical background for one lyric, 'the absolutely revolting "Medical Love Song" ': 'My penile warts, your herpes / My syphilitic sores . . . / At least we both were lying / When we said that we were clear. . . .' Palin sings a couple of songs, including 'Decomposing Composers' ('You can say what you like to Debussy / There's very little left of him to hear'). . . .

'It's funny', Chapman shrugs. 'We don't deliberately set out to offend. Unless we feel it's justified. And in the case of certain well-known religions, it was justified.'

All things dull and ugly
All creatures short and squat
All things rude and nasty
The Lord God made the lot

. . . On the fourth and final night in L. A. the audience is rabid and fanatical, some members dressed in Pythonesque drag. When Cleese walks through the crowd hawking a frozen albatross, half-a-dozen fans answer his cries of 'Albatross!' with 'What flavour is it?' If he had any trouble finding Jones in the crowd, those fans would clearly be willing and able to finish the sketch themselves.

And twice Python receives huge ovations. . . . The first comes in the 'pet shop' sketch. . . . The second comes at the tail end of the show: as one sketch ends, Idle steps to the front of the stage and shouts. 'I didn't ask to do this, you know. This isn't what I really want to do. I want to be a . . . a *lumberjack*!' Idle whips off his jacket to reveal a Pendleton shirt, and the rest of Python troops onstage in Canadian Mountie suits. They begin singing 'The Lumberjack Song', and the Bowl goes crazy.

It's hysterically funny at times, but it's also unsettling. The crowd laughs because it's Python doing their hits, not because they're adding anything to stock routines. . . .

But it's Python together and Python in the flesh – rare occurrences these days. The group has done an exemplary job of following Palin's advice: 'Give the people less and less, and keep them wanting more'.

It's all a far cry from Python's first American appearance, when they came down following a short Canadian tour to perform on the *Tonight Show* in front of an audience completely unfamiliar with them. 'We did an hour's worth of material in twenty minutes', says Idle. 'All the sketches with high, screechy women's voices. *Dead silence.* They did not understand a thing.'

He grins. 'It was great. I mean, that's the reason we all got in the business in the first place: to find something so funny that nobody *dares* laugh.'

Rolling Stone, 13 November 1980.

48 DEATH OF BASIL

Do Not Adjust Your Set (1967-69) was the programme in which two-thirds of Python was constituted (Palin, Jones, Idle and Gilliam – Cleese and Chapman being, you'll recall, in *1948*). George Melly – who later was perhaps the first critic to compare Gilliam's animations to the collages of Max Ernst (Gilliam in his *Film Comment* interview: 'I've also been compared to Max Ernst. I only knew Ernst by name, not by collage. The best thing about reading reviews of yourself is that you discover all the things you missed and so you go out and find kindred spirits. I've got piles of Max Ernst stuff now. His collage work is wonderful') – evokes a prophetic moment.

Another growing cult is the children's show *Do Not Adjust Your Set* (Thames). This is indeed worth catching if you're home by 5.20 on Wednesday evenings. . . . The most inspired lunacy last week was a sketch in which a trades union meeting of gnomes, elves and fairies got side-tracked into an argument as to whether humans existed. Most of the little people thought they didn't, but a leprechaun and a fairy were strongly convinced of our reality. 'If there aren't people', asked the fairy, 'who makes Frank Sinatra records?' 'They are sent from above from whence or for what purpose we know not', parried a sententious gnome. Undefeated she came back with another piece of evidence. 'Who trod on Basil, the mad stoat?' she asked triumphantly. The children thought I'd do myself an injury.

Observer, 30 March 1969.

PYTHONOGRAPHY
Compiled by Lucy Douch

TELEVISION

That Was The Week That Was (BBC-1)

1st Series: 24 November 1962 to 27 April 1963
2nd Series: 28 September 1963 to 21 December 1963
That Was The Year That Was on 29 December 1962 and 28 December 1963
Produced and directed by Ned Sherrin. Regular cast: David Kernan, Roy Kinnear, William Rushton, Kenneth Cope, Lance Percival, Millicent Martin, with David Frost as link-man. Written contributions from **John Cleese**.

Now (TWW)

1966
Teenage pop programme presented by **Michael Palin**.

Frost Report (BBC-1)

1st Series: 10 March 1966 to 28 April 1966
(1) on Authority (2) on Holidays (3) on Sin (4) on Elections (5) on Class (6) on The News (7) on Education (8) on Love
2nd Series: 6 April 1967 to 18 May 1967
(1) on Money (2) on Women (3) on The Forces (4) untitled (5) on Parliament (6) on The Countryside (7) on Industry
Frost Over Christmas 26 December 1967
Starring David Frost, with Ronnie Barker, Ronnie Corbett, **John Cleese**, Sheila Steafel, Julie Felix
Written contributions from **John Cleese** (material sometimes co-written with **Graham Chapman**), **Michael Palin** and **Terry Jones**, and **Eric Idle.**
Prod James Gilbert.

Isadora: The Biggest Dancer in the World (BBC-1)

22 September 1966
Starring Vivian Pickles
Produced and directed by Ken Russell
Uncredited appearances by **Michael Palin** and **Eric Idle** as members of a jazz band playing on the roof of a hearse.

The Late Show (BBC-1)

15 October 1966 to 17 December 1966, and 5 January 1967 to 1 April 1967
Prod Hugh Burnett (Jack Gold from 14 January 1967)
Michael Palin and **Terry Jones** wrote material and appeared.

The Frost Programme (Rediffusion Network)

19 October 1966 to 4 January 1967
Presented by David Frost
Prog Eds **John Cleese**, Tim Brooke-Taylor, Bryan Fitzjones, Michael Gowers, Peter Baker *Dir* Ian Fordyce *Prod* Geoffrey Hughes.

Alice in Wonderland (BBC-1)

28 December 1966
Directed and produced by Jonathan Miller
With Alan Bennett, John Bird, Wilfrid Brambell, Peter Cook, Sir John Gielgud, Malcolm Muggeridge, Sir Michael Redgrave, Peter Sellers and brief, uncredited appearance by **Eric Idle.**

At Last the 1948 Show (Rediffusion)

1st Series: 15 February 1967 to 22 March 1967
2nd Series: 26 September 1967 to 7 November 1967
Written and performed by Tim Brooke-Taylor, **John Cleese, Graham Chapman,** Marty Feldman, with Aimi Macdonald
Exec Prod David Frost *Dir* Ian Fordyce *Prod Eds* **John Cleese** and Tim Brooke-Taylor.

Frost Over England (BBC-1)

26 March 1967
Compilation of Frost Reports for BBC's entry for the Montreux Festival 1967, including sketches with **John Cleese.**

A Series of Bird's (BBC-1)

3 October 1967 to 21 November 1967
Written by John Bird and John Fortune
Prod Dennis Main Wilson
Additional material by **Michael Palin** and **Terry Jones.**

Twice a Fortnight (BBC-1)
21 October 1967 to 23 December 1967
With Bill Oddie, Jonathan Lynn, Graeme Garden and Dilys Watling, plus **Michael Palin** and **Terry Jones**
Introduced by Ronald Fletcher. Produced and directed by Tony Palmer.

No, That's Me Over Here (Rediffusion Network)
14 November 1967 to 19 December 1967
Starring Ronnie Corbett
Written by Barry Cryer, **Graham Chapman** and **Eric Idle**
Exec Prod David Frost *Prod* Bill Hitchcock and Marty Feldman.

Do Not Adjust Your Set
1st Series: (Rediffusion Network) 4 January 1968 to 28 March 1968
2nd Series: (Thames Television) 19 February 1969 to 14 May 1969
Starring Denise Coffey, **Eric Idle,** David Jason, **Terry Jones, Michael Palin**
Written by **Eric Idle, Terry Jones** and **Michael Palin**
Prod Humphrey Barclay (1st series) Ian Davidson (2nd series)
Dir Daphne Shadwell (1st series) Adrian Cooper (2nd series)
Do Not Adjust Your Stocking 26 December 1968.

Marty (BBC-2)
1st Series 29 April 1968 to 3 June 1968
2nd Series 9 December 1968 to 13 January 1969
Starring Marty Feldman
Additional material by **John Cleese, Graham Chapman, Terry Jones** and **Michael Palin** (1st series)
Written by **John Cleese** and **Graham Chapman, Terry Jones** and **Michael Palin** (2nd series)
Prod Dennis Main Wilson *Dir* Roger Race.

We Have Ways of Making You Laugh (London Weekend Television)
23 August 1968 to 18 October 1968
Presented by Frank Muir *Prod* Humphrey Barclay *Dir* Bill Turner
Terry Gilliam resident cartoonist. Written material and appearances by **Eric Idle.**

Broaden Your Mind (BBC-2)
28 October 1968 to 2 December 1968
Starring Tim Brooke-Taylor and Graeme Garden
Additional material from **John Cleese, Graham Chapman, Eric Idle, Terry Jones** and **Michael Palin**
Guest appearances by **Terry Jones, Michael Palin** and **Graham Chapman.**

The Complete and Utter History of Britain (London Weekend Television)
12 January 1969 to 16 February 1969
1. From the Dawn of History to the Normal Conquest
2. Richard the Lionheart to Robin the Hood
3. Edward the First to Richard the Last
4. Perkin Warbeck to Bloody Mary
5. The Great and Glorious Age of Elizabeth
6. James the McFirst to Oliver Cromwell

Starring **Michael Palin** and **Terry Jones** plus Wallace Eaton, Colin Gordon, Roddy Maude-Roxby, Melinda Maye and Diana Quick
Dir Maurice Murphy *Prod* Humphrey Barclay. Written by **Michael Palin** and **Terry Jones.**

Doctor in the House (London Weekend Television)
12 July 1969
'Why do you want to be a Doctor?' by **John Cleese** and **Graham Chapman**
Based on the 'Doctor' books by Richard Gordon
Starring Barry Evans *Dir* David Askey *Prod* Humphrey Barclay.

Monty Python's Flying Circus (BBC-1)
1st Series: 5 October 1969 to 26 October 1969, and 23 November 1969 to 11 January 1970
2nd Series: 15 September 1970 to 29 September 1970, and 20 October 1970 to 22 December 1970
3rd Series: 19 October 1972 to 21 December 1972, and 4 January 1973 to 18 January 1973
Conceived and written by **Graham Chapman, John Cleese, Eric Idle, Terry Jones** and **Michael Palin** *Dir* Ian McNaughton *Prod* John Howard Davies
Animations by **Terry Gilliam**
4th Series: **Monty Python** (BBC-2) 31 October 1974 to 5 December 1974

Conceived and written by **Graham Chapman, Terry Gilliam, Eric Idle, Terry Jones** and **Michael Palin** *Dir* Ian McNaughton *Prod* John Howard Davies.

Late Night Line Up (BBC-2)
12 January 1970
Presented by Joan Bakewell, Michael Dean, Tony Bilbow and Sheridan Morley
Ed Rowan Ayers *Prod* Mike Fentiman
Guests: **John Cleese, Graham Chapman, Terry Gilliam, Eric Idle** and Carol Cleveland.

The Marty Feldman Comedy Machine (ATV)
8 October 1971 to 14 January 1972
Dir John Robins *Prod* Larry Gilbert *Exec Prod* Colin Clews
Animations by **Terry Gilliam.**

Elementary, My Dear Watson (BBC-1)
Comedy Playhouse 18 January 1973
Written by N.F. Simpson
Starring **John Cleese** as Sherlock Holmes and William Rushton as Dr Watson
Prod Barry Took *Dir* Harold Snoad.

Doctor at Large/In Charge (London Weekend Television)
Various episodes throughout 1972 and 1973 written by **John Cleese** and co-written (with Bernard McKenna/David Sherlock) by **Graham Chapman**
Of special interest: 'No Ill Feelings' by **John Cleese**, 3 February 1973, featuring Timothy Bateson as Basil Fawlty prototype
Dir Alan Wallis *Exec Prod* Humphrey Barclay.

Secrets (BBC-2)
Black and Blue drama series, 14 August 1973
Written by **Michael Palin** and **Terry Jones**
Starring Warren Mitchell *Dir* James Cellan Jones *Prod* Mark Shivas.

Monty Pythons fliegende Zirkus (BBC-2)
6 October 1973
Special German edition 'Schnapps with Everything'
Prod Thomas Woitkewitsch of Bavarian Atelier GmbH Munich for WDR.

The Do-It-Yourself Film Animation Show (BBC-1)
5 May 1974
Programme 3: 'Table top and cut-out animation'
Guest **Terry Gilliam**
Presented by Bob Godfrey *Dir* Anna Jackson *Prod* David Hargreaves.

In Vision (BBC-2)
6 December 1974
William Hardcastle meets Monty Python: a look back over five years of Monty Python's Flying Circus with some extracts from some of the best and worst moments
With **Graham Chapman, Terry Gilliam, Terry Jones** and **Michael Palin**
Prod Peter Foges *Ed* Will Wyatt.

Rutland Weekend Television (BBC-2)
1st Series: 12 May 1975 to 16 June 1975
'Christmas with Rutland Weekend Television' 26 December 1975
2nd Series: 12 November 1976 to 24 December 1976
Written by **Eric Idle** *Dir* Andrew Gosling *Prod* Ian Keill
Featuring **Eric Idle,** Neil Innes.

Fawlty Towers (BBC-2)
1st Series: 19 September 1975 to 24 October 1975
2nd Series: 19 February 1979 to 18 March 1979, and 25 October 1979
Written by **John Cleese** and Connie Booth
Starring **John Cleese,** Prunella Scales, Andrew Sachs and Connie Booth
Prod John Howard Davies (1st series), Douglas Argent (2nd series).

The Selling Line (BBC-2) Video Arts Ltd
6 October 1975 to 24 November 1975
Series written by **John Cleese** and Tony Jay
Featuring **John Cleese**
1. Who Sold You This, Then?
2. It's Alright, It's Only a Customer
3. The Competitive Spirit
4. In Two Minds
5. Awkward Customers
6. More Awkward Customers
7. I'll Think About It
8. How Not To Exhibit Yourself.

Three Men in a Boat (BBC-2)
31 December 1975
Starring **Michael Palin**, Tim Curry and Stephen Moore
Prod Rosemary Hill *Dir* Stephen Frears.

Tomkinson's Schooldays (BBC-2)
7 January 1976
Written by **Michael Palin** and **Terry Jones**
Produced and directed by Terry Hughes
Starring **Michael Palin,** with **Terry Jones.**

Festival 40 (BBC-1)
16 August 1976
Monty Python's Flying Circus – special edition conceived, written and performed by **Graham Chapman, John Cleese, Terry Gilliam, Eric Idle, Terry Jones** and **Michael Palin**
Prod Ian McNaughton
Graham Chapman remembers Monty Python, interviewed by David Gillard.

The Strange Case of the End of Civilization As We Know It (London Weekend Television)
18 September 1977
Written by Jack Hobbs, Joseph McGrath and **John Cleese**
Starring **John Cleese** as A. Sherlock-Holmes, Arthur Lowe and Connie Booth
Dir Joseph McGrath *Prod* Humphrey Barclay.

Ripping Yarns (BBC-2)
1st Series: 20 September 1977 to 25 October 1977
1. Tomkinson's Schooldays (dir Terry Hughes)
2. The Testing of Eric Olthwaite (dir Jim Franklin)
3. Escape from Stalag Luft 112B (dir Terry Hughes)
4. Murder at Moorstones Manor (dir Terry Hughes)
5. Across the Andes by Frog (dir Terry Hughes)
6. The Curse of the Claw (dir Jim Franklin)

2nd Series: 10 October 1979 to 24 October 1979
1. Whinfrey's Last Stand (dir Alan J.W. Bell)
2. Golden Gordon (dir Alan J.W. Bell)
3. Roger of the Raj (dir Alan J.W. Bell)

Written by **Michael Palin** and **Terry Jones.**

The Muppet Show (ATV)
21 October 1977
Guest **John Cleese**
Dir Philip Casson *Prod* Jim Henson.

The Rutles (BBC-2)
27 March 1978
Conceived and written by **Eric Idle**
Music and lyrics by Neil Innes. *Dir* Gary Weis and **Eric Idle**
Featuring **Eric Idle, Michael Palin,** Neil Innes, Mick Jagger, Ron Wood.

The Pythons (BBC-1)
20 June 1979
Documentary to commemorate the 10th anniversary of the 'best known British comedy group in the world'
Produced and narrated by Iain Johnstone.

Friday Night, Saturday Morning (BBC-2)
9 November 1979
Presented by Tim Rice
Discussion between **John Cleese, Michael Palin,** Malcolm Muggeridge and Dr Mervyn Stockwood about *Monty Python's Life of Brian*
Dir John Burrowes *Prod* Iain Johnstone.

The Taming of the Shrew (BBC-2)
23 October 1980
'BBC Television Shakespeare' series
Produced and directed by Jonathan Miller
Starring **John Cleese** and Sarah Badel.

Confessions of a Train-Spotter (BBC-2)
27 November 1980
4th in a series of seven 'Great Railway Journeys of the World'
Featuring **Michael Palin**
Prod Ken Stephinson *Series Prod* Roger Laughton.

FILMS

Interlude (1967) *dir* Kevin Billington
Starring Oscar Werner, Barbara Ferris and Virginia Maskell, with **John Cleese** as a television PR man.

Albert Carter Q.O.S.O. (1968) Dormer Productions
Short film starring Roy Kinnear with **Eric Idle.**

The Magic Christian (1969) *dir* Joseph McGrath
Starring Peter Sellers and Ringo Starr, with **John Cleese** as a director of Sotheby's and **Graham Chapman** as an Oxford stroke
Screenplay by **Graham Chapman, John Cleese,** Peter Sellers, Terry Southern and Joseph McGrath.

The Rise and Rise of Michael Rimmer (1969) *dir* Kevin Billington
Starring Vanessa Redgrave, Peter Cook, Denholm Elliott, Ronald Fraser, Arthur Lowe and **John Cleese**
Screenplay by **Graham Chapman, John Cleese,** Peter Cook and Kevin Billington.

The Cry of the Banshee (1970) *dir* Gordon Hessler
Starring Vincent Price and Elisabeth Bergner, with an uncredited appearance by **Terry Gilliam.**

Doctor in Trouble (1970) *dir* Ralph Thomas
Starring Leslie Phillips, Harry Secombe and James Robertson Justice, with **Graham Chapman** as Roddy.

The Statue (1970) *dir* Rod Amateau
Starring David Niven, Virna Lisi, Robert Vaughn and Ann Bell, with **John Cleese** as Harry, a renegade psychiatrist.

And Now For Something Completely Different (1971) *dir* Ian McNaughton
Written by and featuring **John Cleese, Graham Chapman, Eric Idle, Terry Jones** and **Michael Palin**
Animations by **Terry Gilliam.**

The Love Ban/It's a 2' 6'' Above the Ground World (1972) *dir* Ralph Thomas
Starring Hwyel Bennett, Nanette Newman, Milo O'Shea and **John Cleese.**

Monty Python and the Holy Grail (1974) *dir* **Terry Jones** and **Terry Gilliam**
Written by and featuring **John Cleese, Graham Chapman, Eric Idle, Terry Jones** and **Michael Palin**
Animations by **Terry Gilliam.**

Romance with a Double Bass (1974) *dir* Robert Young
Starring **John Cleese** and Connie Booth
Screen adaptation from Chekhov by **John Cleese** with Connie Booth and Robert Young.

Pleasure at Her Majesty's (1976) *dir* Roger Graef
With Alan Bennett, John Bird, Eleanor Bron, Tim Brooke-Taylor, **John Cleese,** Peter Cook, Bill Oddie, John Fortune.

Jabberwocky (1977) *dir* **Terry Gilliam**
Starring **Michael Palin** as Dennis Cooper, Max Wall, John le Mesurier, Warren Mitchell and Harry H Corbett, with **Terry Jones** as a poacher.

The Odd Job (1978) *dir* Peter Medak
Starring **Graham Chapman** as Arthur Harris, and David Jason
Written and co-produced by **Graham Chapman.**

Monty Python's Life of Brian (1979) *dir* **Terry Jones**
Written by and featuring **John Cleese, Graham Chapman, Eric Idle, Terry Jones** and **Michael Palin** with **Terry Gilliam.**

The Secret Policeman's Ball (1979) *dir* Roger Graef
With Rowan Atkinson, Ken Campbell, **John Cleese,** Peter Cook, **Michael Palin,** Pete Townshend, John Williams
Stage direction by **John Cleese.**

The Great Muppet Caper (1981) *dir* Jim Henson
Starring Charles Grodin, Diana Rigg with **John Cleese.**

Time Bandits (1981) *dir* **Terry Gilliam**
Starring Sean Connery, Shelley Duvall, Ian Holm, **John Cleese,** David Warner and Craig Warnock.

The Secret Policeman's Other Ball (1982) *dir* Julian Temple

With Rowan Atkinson, Alan Bennett, **Graham Chapman, John Cleese,** Billy Connolly, John Fortune, Alexei Sayle, Pamela Stephenson, John Wells.

Guest appearance by **Michael Palin.**

BOOKS

Monty Python's Big Red Book/Eyre Methuen 1971.

The Brand New Monty Python Bok/Eyre Methuen 1973 (issued in paperback as *The Brand New Monty Python Papperbok*/Eyre Methuen 1974).

Monty Python and the Holy Grail (Book)/Edited by Terry Jones/Designed by Derek Birdsall/Eyre Methuen 1977

Monty Python's Life of Brian/Edited by Eric Idle/Designed by Basil Pao/Eyre Methuen 1979

The Complete Works of Shakespeare and Monty Python: Volume One – Monty Python/Eyre Methuen 1981 (combined re-issue of *Monty Python's Big Red Book* and *The Brand New Monty Python Bok*)

Bert Fegg's Nasty Book for Boys and Girls/Terry Jones and Michael Palin/Eyre Methuen 1974

Rutland Dirty Weekend Book/Eric Idle/Eyre Methuen 1976

Hello Sailor/Eric Idle/Futura 1976

The Strange Case of the End of Civilization as We Know It/John Cleese and Jack Hobbs/Star Books 1977

Fawlty Towers/John Cleese and Connie Booth/Contact Publications 1977

Animations of Mortality/Terry Gilliam/Eyre Methuen 1978

Ripping Yarns/Terry Jones and Michael Palin/Eyre Methuen 1978

Fawlty Towers Book 2/John Cleese and Connie Booth/Weidenfeld and Nicolson 1979

More Ripping Yarns/Terry Jones and Michael Palin/Eyre Methuen 1980

A Liar's Autobiography/Graham Chapman/Eyre Methuen 1980

Chaucer's Knight – the Portrait of a Medieval Mercenary/Terry Jones/Weidenfeld and Nicolson 1980

Fairy Tales/Terry Jones/Illustrated by Michael Foreman/Pavilion Books 1981